TREE TOP

TREE TOP

CREATING A FRUIT REVOLUTION

David H. Stratton

WSU PRESS

Washington State University Press
Pullman, Washington

Washington State University Press
PO Box 645910
Pullman, Washington 99164-5910
Phone: 800-354-7360
Fax: 509-335-8568
Email: wsupress@wsu.edu
Website: wsupress.wsu.edu

Library of Congress Cataloging-in-Publication Data

Stratton, David H. (David Hodges), 1927-
    Tree Top : creating a fruit revolution / David H. Stratton.
        p. cm.
    Includes bibliographical references and index.
    ISBN 978-0-87422-306-4 (alk. paper)
    1. Tree Top, Inc.--History. 2. Apple industry—Washington (State)—History. 3. Fruit trade—Washington (State)—
History. I. Title.
    HD9259.A6T747 2010
    338.7'6636309797—dc22   2010014484

Fine Quality Books from the Pacific Northwest

Contents

Foreword

For 50 years Tree Top has evolved to meet the changing conditions of the Pacific Northwest processing industry. For most of that time, the cooperative has operated with a policy of accepting all the processing fruit that a member delivered. As new acreages of trees were planted, Tree Top expanded its fruit-processing capacity. Also, the cooperative has pursued a consistent strategy of adding new products and acquiring additional plants and facilities to increase marketing opportunities and profits for the grower-members. A highly competitive domestic marketplace and, more recently, "flooding" of the international arena with vast supplies of inexpensive apple juice concentrate have challenged Tree Top to perform more efficiently and innovatively.

In the face of these changes and many others in the fruit-growing and fruit-processing business, Tree Top has had to continually examine and re-define the strategic plans involving its position and direction in the industry. Profitability in the form of returns to its members and, ultimately, viability in a tough competitive environment, have been major concerns. As a result, the 2009 crop year was the first time Tree Top limited fruit deliveries of its members. This policy may well be a solution to the cooperative's problem of matching the raw product delivered for processing with the demands of the marketplace.

For the past half-century, Tree Top has made adjustments to meet changes at home and on the international scene. The cooperative's board of directors, management team, and employees have been, and will continue to be, dedicated to creating value for fruit in a global marketplace filled with over-capacity.

Tom Auvil
Chairman, Board of Directors

Acres of apple crates.

Preface

In the popular mind apples evoke an image of Washington state, just as oranges mean Florida and pineapples suggest Hawaii.[1] And rightly so, because Washington is the number one apple grower in the Union. The Evergreen State can also claim another distinction among its bragging rights. Tree Top Inc., an agricultural cooperative with several fruit product lines, is one of the largest processors of apples and pears in the world. Yet the location of its headquarters is not the state's famous seaport and largest city, Seattle, nor the eastside metropolis, Spokane, nor even the well-known interior city of Yakima, but in the nearby bustling small town of Selah. Such a locale might seem inconsistent with a global business status. In fact, though, Tree Top has pitched its major marketing and advertising program on the basis of time-honored, small-town values familiar in Selah, and presumably all across America. So, the firm has always taken pride in "the warmth and country feel" of its business operations.

For example, the front label on a one-gallon container of "Tree Top 100% Apple Juice" bears the firm's main promotional message: "Real Fruit from Real People." Another label on the back of the bottle carries a homey, personal statement from the cooperative's 1,062 grower-owners in Washington, Oregon, and Idaho:

For over 50 years we have held true to our small town heritage of care, craftsmanship, and quality. As the growers of Tree Top, we take pride in sharing the wholesome goodness of pure fruit in every glass. And as the owners of the company, we sincerely thank you for enjoying the fruits of our labor.

How well such up-front, folksy, small-town values have resonated during the past half century for an agricultural cooperative headquartered in rural Selah, Washington, but competing in a world increasingly influenced by big-city mass marketing, dot-com technology, and globalization, is the subject of this book.

William H. "Bill" Charbonneau owned and operated Tree Top before it got that name and became a cooperative in 1960, and he continued as its general manager, or CEO,

for another five years. A driven perfectionist, Charbonneau influenced the firm's future course long after his departure, particularly in maintaining rigid standards of quality, purity, and taste. Previously, while employed as a salesman in Portland, he had become dissatisfied with selling "fruit drinks" that actually contained only 15 percent real juice. In his view these beverages were only "belly wash" masquerading as the real thing. When Charbonneau obtained his own company, he bucked the general trend of that day by proudly marketing apple juice that included no refined sugar.[2] Besides his obsession with high product standards, he also developed a visionary plan of expansion in fruit processing.

Today, in fulfillment of Charbonneau's vision, Tree Top's seven plants produce apple juice and cider as the backbone of its retail market in 30 states, with the core outlets in the West and Southwest, and also distribute consumer packaged goods, such as fresh apple slices, blends with other juices, and apple sauce. In addition, the cooperative sells as bulk "ingredients" a wide variety of dried and frozen fruit products as well as juice concentrates and purees used by the international and domestic food industries. As a legacy of Bill Charbonneau's high standards and disdain for diluted products, the label on a contemporary jar of Tree Top apple sauce bears the words "Natural" and "No Sugar Added."

In 1951, *Life* magazine ran a pictorial article that showed a bulldozer shoving discarded apples into a mountainous pile at the Yakima city dump. Pigs rooted around in the mess as a choking stench rose to the heavens. Local orchardists blamed their losses, once valued at $6 million, on distant unseen forces, such as the value of the dollar, restrictive tariffs, and the collapse of foreign markets. Federal subsidies, they declared, were the only solution for their troubles.[3] From its beginning, however, Tree Top's mission has been to solve exactly that problem. In effect, the cooperative set out "to make something out of nothing"—to take the "culls," or low-grade but otherwise perfectly good fruit once considered as un-saleable, and give

Culls taken to the Chelan dump, 1950s. Scenes like this were common before the development of apple juice as an important marketplace commodity.

them significant value. As a company publication reminded orchardists in 1973:

Some of us…can remember when you didn't have to bother about your culls—you simply dumped them, probably at the county or city dump. Some of us who live a few miles out in apple growing areas can remember all too well the dump trucks from warehouses going by on their way to the dump—dripping and accompanied by the inevitable swarms of flies. The only return growers got in those days was the flies who soon returned from the dump to pester households in the area. The only "home" then for those tons of culls was the dump and a fourth of your potential profit poured over the tailgate of a dump truck; in fact, sometimes it was a third of your profit.[4]

Since the founding of Tree Top, the article pointed out, its grower-members had seen their previously worthless culls bring them financial returns year after year. A later Tree Top executive put it in the terms of an old folk-saying: "We are making a silk purse out of a sow's ear."[5]

In this vein the cooperative's primary responsibility has been to open as many opportunities as possible for the orchardists to sell their crops, whether it meant developing new products, establishing more marketing outlets, or building or acquiring additional production facilities. In fact, driven by this mission, one of the firm's outstanding attributes has been its continual search for new possibilities of diversification. Later, just as it had done for apples, Tree Top created a market for cull pears when none had really existed before, thus recording another significant contribution to the financial structure of the larger fruit industry. Such a mission, that emphasizes expansion and diversification, has kept Tree Top management on the alert to try out new projects, often with success, but sometimes with the opposite results. A private corporation making only one product, or a relative few, might have the option of saying, in effect, we are big enough and this is as far as we need to go. Not so for Tree Top—it has been under an unrelenting challenge to take on big, new ventures and promote new product lines. There has been little free time for reflection on past accomplishments.

Tree Top has had a history of ups and downs followed by creative adjustments, careful restructuring, and innovative reorientation. As board chair Roger Strand stated in the 1991 annual report, "Each year seems to be uniquely difficult in our business." But the most worrisome problem of all has been the fluctuating supply of raw product, mostly apples, available for processing. This dilemma has been influential, if not decisive, in most of the firm's major policy shifts, successes, and setbacks. Neither Bill Charbonneau nor his successors could ever control this supply pipeline with absolute certainty. Charbonneau tried to solve the problem by selling his privately owned company to the Tree Top cooperative, whose orchardist-owners made contracts to furnish fruit to the firm they had created. These contractual agreements would supposedly stabilize the flow of the raw product. It was a wonderful idea, but, as it turned out, not foolproof because of such uncertainties as smaller crops than expected and other factors.

For instance, harsh weather and attacks of insects and disease in the orchards could make life difficult for the processors, who had to take the culls and "sortouts" left-over from the fresh-fruit trade. It was difficult to open new markets or make promises of delivery to established outlets when the vagaries of the raw material available determined the volume of production. As one company executive commented in 1978, "If the apples were available to us, we do not know how much [of our products] we could sell."[6] Almost 30 years later, in 2007, when hail damage and discoloration of apples seemed to promise a large supply for processing, the low-grade fruit normally available went instead to grocery stores and produce stands for sale at bargain prices. At the bottom of the marketing chain, Tree Top's share of processor apples was the smallest it had received in several years.

Nevertheless, Tree Top has faithfully fulfilled its mission, but not without taking some chances and weathering some threatening storms. For instance, one of Bill Charbonneau's pioneering contributions to the apple industry as a whole was his introduction of frozen concentrated juice in Washington. The process had been used for other fruit, notably by the citrus business of Florida, but only on a small scale for apples. The new product brought immediate consumer

Apples and Apple Cider
An American Tradition

From Adam and Eve in the Garden of Eden to Snow White eating a poisoned red fruit, the apple has been surrounded by spiritual and romantic mysticism. Throw in Johnny Appleseed and the national fixation with apple pie, and the legendary aspects include the main elements of American folklore.

Yet, on the side of practicality, as one historian has observed, "No other fruit could be started so easily, nor could be put to so many essential uses."[1] In fact, from the beginning of European settlement in America, apples were considered an absolute necessity. They could be stored in cellars for leisurely snacks around a fireplace during cold winter nights, dried and kept for eating and pie-making, canned as preserves or a butter, or made into cider and vinegar. In a time when polluted streams and cisterns often spread disease, hard cider, or applejack, was often more popular than water to quench a thirst.[2] In particular, vinegar served many medicinal purposes, ranging from cough syrup to a cure for acne, and, in a mixture with molasses, as a remedy for hair loss and a tonic for the relief of seasonal doldrums, especially "spring fever." By tradition no pioneer farm seemed complete unless it had a certain number of apple trees allotted to meet the needs of each and every family member.

1. Robert Price, *Johnny Appleseed: Man and Myth* (Bloomington: Indiana University Press, 1954), 39, quoted in Amanda L. Van Lanen, "'We Have Grown Fine Fruit Whether We Would or No': The History of the Washington State Apple Industry, 1880–1930," Ph.D. dissertation, Washington State University, 2009, 18. Most of the information used in this sidebar comes from Van Lanen's study.
2. Modern products labeled "Apple Juice" are customarily pasteurized. Products bearing the label "Apple Cider" or "Sweet Cider" are usually unfiltered and unfermented (non-alcoholic) apple juice, which may be pasteurized. So-called "Hard Cider" or "Country Cider" are fermented or partially fermented and often not pasteurized.

The Magic Wand of the Railroads

Early commercial fruit cultivation in Washington east of the Cascade Range served only local markets because of the limited transportation facilities available, principally wagons and river steamboats. In the 1880s, however, this restricted situation quickly changed when the Northern Pacific Railroad forged a transcontinental link across eastern Washington and, eventually, up the Yakima Valley and over the Cascades to Tacoma. The Northern Pacific and later, in the 1890s, the Great Northern Railway, which serviced the Wenatchee Valley, offered access to national sales outlets. The railroads also promoted fruit growing and large-scale irrigation, often owning a controlling interest in the water enterprises.[1]

The magic wand of the railroads brought spectacular results. About 1886, Philip Miller, an early miner turned orchardist, had planted the first apple trees in the Wenatchee Valley, having transported them on mule back from The Dalles, Oregon. By 1909, the Great Northern was shipping out more than 2,000 boxcars of apples from Wenatchee, while, in 1907, the Northern Pacific had shipped over $1 million worth of fruit, mostly apples, from the Yakima Valley. By the 1930s, one out of every eight apples grown in the United States came from the Wenatchee-Okanogan area and 17,000 carloads of apples were being shipped out annually. This part of north-central Washington could boast that it produced more apples than any other area of comparable size in the world.[2] While the fresh-apple trade flourished, the processing of "culls" had started, but only on a relatively small scale.

In the summer of 1892, Great Northern Railway construction crews laid tracks through the Wenatchee Valley. To the west, in the Cascade Mountains, crews built a series of switchback tracks to ascend the crest. The Great Northern was completed to Puget Sound in January 1893, and arrived in Seattle in June. Along with the earlier Northern Pacific Railroad, Washington's apple country now had two transcontinental rail links with major national markets. Pictured here are two Great Northern locomotives of the 1890s on the switchbacks along the eastern slopes of Stevens Pass.

Courtesy of the BNSF Railway

---

1. The love-hate relationship between the apple growers and the railroads is discussed in Van Lanen, "We Have Grown Fine Fruit," 205–6.
2. Otis W. Freeman, "Apple Industry of the Wenatchee Area," *Economic Geography* 10 (April 1934), 160–71.

Charbonneau Tree Top pure frozen concentrated apple juice.

repercussions helped ¬ Tree Top president to lose his job, and in recovering from the Alar crisis, the cooperative barely survived what was probably the most trying time in its history.

Generally, and again related to the supply pipeline, Tree Top has almost literally agonized over whether or not to operate as a "full-service processor," that is, whether or not to pledge that it would take all the fruit the members wanted to deliver every year. Taking it all was fine in short harvests, but caused problems of extra operational expenses and excess carryover inventory with bumper crops. It was "feast or famine," when the ideal was a regular, steady flow of raw product. A companion dilemma, usually prevalent in short harvest years, involved member loyalty to the cooperative; that is, getting the contracted growers to send their culls to Tree Top instead of shopping around for a better price elsewhere. The member contracts were legal documents, but enforcing them in court would almost certainly create a disaster in public relations. Persuasion, not litigation, orchestrated by frequent explanations of the cooperative's benefits over the long haul, became the long-time practice of Tree Top management.

In the latest strategy on these issues, in 2008 the Tree Top board and management team decided to change from the position of being prepared "to take it all" and instead "to maximize returns." This switch called for the strictest efficiency and economy at a fixed level of production, no matter how large the harvest, and also a firm commitment by the growers to deliver the needed raw product. Renegotiated grower contracts spelled out in detail membership responsibility under the new policy. Henceforth, the emphasis would be placed on marketing and profitability, and on giving members the highest returns, but on a regulated, cost-effective manufacturing schedule.

On the global scene Tree Top has opened markets in numerous foreign countries, tried joint ventures in such places as Japan, and taken an active role in issues related to American foreign policy, especially restrictive tariff policies. In particular, the rise of China in a relatively short

acceptance and significant profits for the cooperative. Yet some insider skeptics had opposed this departure from traditional processing operations as too risky and expensive. As a result, Charbonneau got some unpleasant criticism at the same time he was praised for his notable achievement.

In a different kind of challenge, the Alar crisis of the late 1980s and early 1990s brought financial ruin to large segments of the apple industry, and hampered Tree Top for a time. The popular television program *60 Minutes* ran two episodes claiming that Alar, a spray used by orchardists to brighten the color and extend the branch life of apples, caused cancer. Movie star Meryl Streep joined the media crusade as did *Time* and *Newsweek*. Tree Top had conscientiously struggled for the previous three years to ban the use of Alar-treated fruit in any of its branded products, but these efforts made no difference in the harmful effects of the media bombast. Sales of apples and all apple products plummeted. The turmoil faded away, but not before bringing widespread financial distress to individual orchardists and to business concerns such as Tree Top. In fact, the time as the world's largest producer of apples and its alleged dumping of concentrate on the international market have involved the cooperative in a continuing competitive struggle. Mainly, however, the personal relationships inherent in the cooperative concept have dominated the story line during Tree Top's first 50 years. The dynamics of a triangular arrangement beginning with a multitude of grower-owners, who are represented by a 12-member board of directors, who, in turn, give orders to a CEO, have sometimes caused stresses and strains, but have more often worked well. Along the way, Tree Top could take pride in helping make Washington the number one apple state by developing a significant marketing outlet for previously discarded fruit and, in its primary mission of diversification, branching out into several other product lines as well.

An economic-geographical study celebrating Washington's statehood centennial in 1989 summed it up neatly:

Perhaps more than any other branch of agriculture, fruit farming has been transformed by the many technological and socio-economic changes that have influenced farming in the past century. Irrigation, refrigeration, hybridization and other genetic research, fertilizers, herbicides and pesticides, improved harvesting methods and machinery, superior packaging and more effective marketing, not to mention changes in diet and income, have all played a role in making Washington's fruit farming industry one of the most successful in the world.[7]

Tree Top, as an integral part of the fruit industry, has been influenced by all of these changes—and more—during its first half century. 🍎

Endnotes

1. For a personalized tour of Washington's "apple country," see David Guterson, "The Kingdom of Apples: Picking the Fruit of Immortality in Washington's Laden Orchards," *Harper's Magazine*, October 1999, 41–56.
2. *Yakima Herald-Republic*, April 12, 1978, 11.
3. "Sad Applesauce: Glut Ends in a $6 Million Mess," *Life*, September 10, 1951, 52.
4. *Tree Topics*, January 22, 1973. After it began in September 1968, this official monthly, or bimonthly, publication for the cooperative's members became the most widely circulated compilation of company news. Unless cited otherwise, the information here and throughout *Tree Top: Creating a Fruit Revolution* was obtained from the Tree Top Inc. Historical Files, which during the preparation of this book were deposited in the Departmental Archives, Department of History, Washington State University, Pullman (hereafter cited as Tree Top Historical Files). Of special importance in these files is a typewritten manuscript, "Tree Top—The Story of Apple Juice," n.d., which provided substantial information in chapters 1 and 2. Although no author is given, it was written sometime in the 1970s by Ernest L. "Ernie" Stafford, who served as Tree Top sales manager, assistant general manager, and interim general manager.
5. President and CEO Dennis Colleran, quoted in *American/Western Fruit Grower*, September 1983.
6. *Tree Topics*, December 1978.
7. James W. Scott, *Washington: A Centennial Atlas* (Bellingham: Center for Pacific Northwest Studies, Western Washington University, 1989), 54.

Chapter 1

Bill Charbonneau's Domain

In the Hollywood film *Jerry Maguire* (1996), actor Tom Cruise, who portrays an abrasive, hard-bargaining agent representing professional athletes, barks out his trademark clincher: "Show me the money!" This soon became a popular phrase. Long before the movie, William Henry "Bill" Charbonneau, the legendary, roughshod "founding father" of the Tree Top fruit processing cooperative, had made a similar money-on-the-barrel-head phrase the centerpiece of his business affairs: "I want my money!" During the 16 years that Charbonneau owned and ran the firm as his private domain, before it became a cooperative in 1960, his accounts receivable seldom went 90 days—many less than 30 days—and a fiscal year ending with even a single bad debt (in one case, only $256) was indeed unusual. On the other hand, he might occasionally be slow to pay some legitimate debts, not out of neglect, but depending on how well he regarded the person to whom he owed money. Above all, Charbonneau was a shrewd businessman with his own set of strict principles.

A stickler for the integrity and high quality of any product connected with his name, Charbonneau had, in a previous job, regularly checked the stated weights on the bathroom paper cartons he sold, and with righteous indignation returned the lighter ones to his employer, a forest products company. At his own firm he was an old-style, hands-on executive, keeping a close watch on every phase of management and production. Once, when an obedient floor manager, following Charbonneau's specific orders, reported the possibility of a flavor problem with a batch of

William Henry "Bill" Charbonneau.
The Goodfruit Grower (May 11, 1978).

apple juice, the boss tasted a sample and ordered the whole lot in the 5,000-gallon holding tank dumped down the sewer. At that time the plant might turn out about 10,000 gallons on a big day. Not surprisingly, Bill Charbonneau was often described as a driven perfectionist.

Many of Charbonneau's closest associates regarded him as eccentric, but they invariably expressed their admiration, even awe, for his business acumen. If he was working in a room with 20 others, it was said, one person would probably get along with him, and even then arguments might flare up. Charbonneau's intense personality sometimes defeated his best-laid plans. In dealings with orchardists and fruit warehouse operators, for instance, he often "turned them off" and made them resist, if not reject, his otherwise well-reasoned proposals. Toward such detractors, according to his philosophy, he only felt required to send out the periodic checks he owed them when he got good and ready to do so, and they deserved nothing more from him. Whatever might have been said about his personal traits, however, Bill Charbonneau was regarded as a tough, successful businessman, with exceptional organizational talents and an expansive vision of the important role he could achieve in fruit processing. And most important, his word was his bond; straight talk was his strong suit.

Born in Cleveland, Ohio, in 1906, Charbonneau headed west seeking financial opportunities as a young man. He worked at various sales jobs in Southern California and then in Portland, where he was employed by a beverage company that sold various soft drinks including fruit

Clifford C. Ross and the Tree Top Plants in Selah

The beginnings of Tree Top go back to 1944 when William H. Charbonneau bought the Pomona Products Company from Clifford C. Ross. This facility produced apple juice, but Cliff Ross also owned an apple-drying firm bearing his name that Tree Top later acquired. Influential in both juicing and fruit dehydration processing, Ross also had assumed military contracts for drying potatoes during World War II.

Of historical interest, in 1925 Ross moved his family from The Dalles, Oregon, to Yakima and took over the management of an established apple-drying plant in Selah. Ross bought the company in 1929, and W.S. LeVan joined him as a partner in 1933. The Ross dried-fruit firm processed Washington, Oregon, and

Clifford C. Ross.
Letty Ann Ginn, West Campbell, Ross Campbell

Idaho apples, selling "Selah" and "New West" brands as extra choice, and the "Rovan" product as choice. The latter brand name came from an abbreviated combination of Ross and LeVan. In 1944, Ross sold the Pomona Products Company to Bill Charbonneau, which became the foundation for the establishment of the Tree Top cooperative in 1960.

After World War II, Ross returned to his main interest, the dehydration of fruit. In September 1969, the Ross installation was destroyed by fire, rebuilt and re-equipped, and then sold to Seneca Foods in 1974. Today, as a part of Tree Top since 1976, the modernized "Ross Plant" is one of the cooperative's two adjoining Selah production sites.

juice.[1] Although his sales record was outstanding, Charbonneau felt uneasy about selling the firm's fruit drinks because they contained mostly artificial flavoring. His experience in Portland, however, did give him an opportunity to size up production and marketing activities in the beverage field. As a result, he started looking around for a "sleeper" fruit drink that had promising sales potential and would not mislead the consumer about its quality, or more specifically, its "purity" and authentic "taste." In 1944 this pursuit brought him to the Yakima Valley apple country in Washington where he found exactly what he wanted.

Apples can be grown in most parts of the Pacific Northwest, but the cultivation of these fruit trees has especially flourished in the deep, sheltered Yakima and Wenatchee valleys along the eastern slopes of the Cascade Range.[2] Running north-south from Canada down into northern California, the towering Cascades constitute the most visible geographical feature of the region. A series of snow-crested volcanic peaks, including Mount Rainier, the tallest at 14,411 feet, and St. Helens, which spewed thick layers of ash over a wide area when it erupted in 1980, give the mountain range the appearance of a long, jagged backbone outlined on the horizon. Nature also bestowed on the

region the Columbia River, which begins in Canada and whose tributaries flowing from Wyoming, Montana, Idaho, Oregon, and Washington make it the mightiest waterway in the western United States.

Nestled in "rain shadows" of the Cascades, which block out the moisture-laden clouds passing overhead from the Pacific Ocean, the Yakima and Wenatchee valleys share a protected, moderate climate, but are relatively arid. Both valleys are blessed, however, by rivers headed down them to the Columbia that provide plentiful water for the irrigation of apple orchards.[3] Apple growing on a major scale began to the north in the Okanogan country and, more recently, in the Columbia Basin Irrigation Project of central Washington with its deep, fertile soil and irrigation water from Grand Coulee Dam. Other important production areas in Washington include Lake Chelan, Spokane, and the Skagit Valley.

By the time Bill Charbonneau arrived in the Yakima Valley in 1944, the federal government had long since taken over many of the private irrigation systems, constructed after the arrival of the transcontinental railroads in the 1880s and 1890s. Several other water supply projects had been built in Washington, which resulted in a great

The Pomona Products plant in Selah, about 1941, just before Charbonneau's purchase.
Tree Top Annual Report (October 1973).

Fruit packers row in Selah.
Lince, The Selah Story (1984).

George W. Brown Packing Company.
Lince, The Selah Story (1984).

expansion of apple growing, particularly along the eastern slopes of the Cascade Range. Not surprisingly, packing and marketing facilities had grown up apace.

In his ambitions to become part of this scene, Charbonneau could have faced a formidable obstacle. Although it was now the last stages of World War II, national business and financial activities still remained under tight wartime controls, sometimes making credit difficult to obtain. Charbonneau undoubtedly had some savings and may have recently received an inheritance—the stories vary—but he probably "jawboned" most of the financial arrangements for his purchase of a small apple juice concern, Pomona Products Company located in Selah, the bustling fruit handling center just north of Yakima. Clifford C. Ross was a major stockholder in this firm and also operated a comparatively large apple-drying plant in Selah, which the Tree Top cooperative later bought. Under different ownership, Pomona Products had moved from Yakima into the "Kerper warehouses" at the south end of Selah's "Fruit Row" in June 1936, and had never been really profitable.[4]

For Charbonneau, as the novice owner of a struggling processing plant with aging machinery, it was a daunting challenge, especially in the uncertainties of a wartime economy. But at least he now had a chance to try out his ideas, and to accomplish something on his own without a boss looking over his shoulder. By a stroke of luck, since he was determined to market a product of the highest quality but lacked the experience to do so, Charbonneau sought the professional advice of a skilled scientist, Dr. Alfred M. Neubert, who

Tree Top headquarters in Selah.
Tree Top Annual Report (October 1973).

Tree Top Headquarters in Selah

The establishment of Tree Top headquarters at Selah came by chance when Bill Charbonneau purchased from Clifford C. Ross a small juice processing operation located there. This facility, now known as the "Selah Plant," became the basis for the creation of Tree Top in 1960. In 1971, the cooperative constructed the initial section of the present headquarters building, making substantial additions to the original structure later. In 1976, Tree Top purchased another, nearby Selah processing facility, also once owned by Ross. This apple-drying installation became known as the "Ross Plant."

By the time Tree Top was founded, the town of Selah, with its "fruit row" of processors, warehouses, and similar operations, had already gained recognition as a prominent distribution center. Historically, by the 1850s or earlier, the area's eventual agricultural importance was indicated by the flourishing "gardens" of Indian leader Owhi in the Wenas Valley, a short distance from Selah toward the mountains.

"Selah" was the name of an Old-Testament city at the time of kings David and Solomon, but the word has a sound similar to the Indian name for a local river.[1] The word itself is difficult to translate from Hebrew, having a liturgical function in music and literature, perhaps something like "Amen" when used following a prayer or religious statement to indicate affirmation or approval.

1. Robert S. Lince, *The Selah Story: History of Selah, East Selah, and Wenas Valley in Yakima County, Washington* (Selah: Selah Valley Optimist Printing, 1984), 77.

had a staff position with the Fruit and Vegetable Laboratory of the U.S. Department of Agriculture at nearby Prosser. Neubert specialized in fruit as well as vegetable processing, and had done research on these operations as practiced in Switzerland, an Old-World pioneer in making apple juice. Cliff Ross had employed Neubert, probably as a consultant. The shared expertise of this knowledgeable scientist undoubtedly helped Charbonneau understand the essential technicalities of his new trade.[5] Some accounts also mention that a "chemist," Carl Weisbord (or Weisbrod), who learned apple processing in Germany, had worked for Pomona Products at Selah. He also may have helped Charbonneau get started.[6] A quick learner, Charbonneau soon began planning to make his company "bigger than Minute Maid," the most popular postwar orange beverage.

Some tough times lay ahead. After the end of the war, Charbonneau systematically replaced all of the old plant equipment and, in 1946, changed the Pomona Products name to the Charbonneau Packing Corporation, although he kept using the New West label. At first he sold a blend processed from Red Delicious and Jonathan apples or Red Delicious, Romes, and/or Winesaps through established brokers to markets in only Washington, Oregon, and Montana. In 1949 cider was added to the lineup, particularly at Halloween. Over and over, Charbonneau hammered away on the necessity of high quality, and that quality also meant cleanliness. His pure, flawless juice, as advertised, had to taste exactly like fresh apples, not like the "belly wash" of his competitors. There were absolutely no excuses if it failed that test.

Such decisions and the implementation of them involved relatively simple management skills, but there was one problem that baffled Charbonneau, and that would eventually lead him to sell his company to a cooperative. In fact, this difficulty has plagued Tree Top throughout its history, and has played an influential, if not decisive, role in most of the firm's setbacks and major policy shifts. Not surprisingly, then, this everlasting headache is a major theme of the Tree Top story.

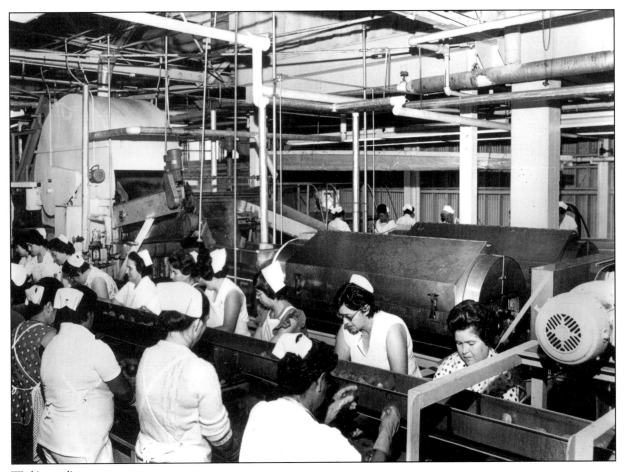

Working on line.

Supply, supply, supply—of raw products, mainly apples—that was what Charbonneau and his successors could never control with any certainty. The main objective of the orchardists in Washington was to grow most of their fruit for the fresh-apple market, and the more the better. During the packing phase in the warehouses, however, sorting took place that removed the "culls," or "sortouts," which in size, shape, or color failed the grading standards for shipping as fresh apples, and which were made available to the apple processors. Two groups of processors—the juice makers and those plants that produced dried fruit—vied for the lowest grades. The dryers usually had a wider range of selection at the warehouses. A juicer such as Charbonneau, because of competitive pricing, had "to make something out of nothing" by taking the leftovers. Actually, to the growers, culls were often regarded as refuse, which they paid to have hauled away and dumped.

In short, Charbonneau and the other processors were seen by many in the apple industry as something like scavengers, who, lurking at the bottom of "the fruit chain," could not enjoy the respect of the fresh-apple trade. If such vagaries as hail, frost, insects, and disease made the growers nervous about the volume their orchards would produce every year, this concern was magnified tenfold for the processors, who always got the short end of the crop.[7] For example, Charbonneau, encouraged by a big apple crop in 1950, expanded from the Northwest into the northern California market area. After initial success, he had to withdraw because a disappointing harvest in 1951 provided only enough culls to supply established outlets with apple juice. As already pointed out, this dilemma would remain as a perpetual challenge for Tree Top. Or, to see it another way, Charbonneau's remarkable success in creating a demand for apple juice often outdistanced his ability to obtain sufficient raw material for processing.

After conducting a name contest among his employees, Charbonneau introduced Tree Top as his main brand in 1947, running expensive ads in the Sunday supplements of Seattle and Los Angeles newspapers that depicted "New West-Tree Top Apple Juice." Consumer response soon clearly indicated, however, that Tree Top alone provided much greater brand recognition. New West remained on the label in smaller letters until 1951 when a new format appeared with "Charbonneau Tree Top." Significantly, after expensive ads ran in the Seattle and Los Angeles newspapers, a short apple crop made it impossible for the company to deliver enough products to satisfy the demand of these markets.

Despite ups and downs in the supply pipeline, increased sales became an obsession of the restless Charbonneau. Until 1955, he depended largely on regional brokers to establish new markets and promote sales. Then he became convinced that recent tree plantings and other conditions would increase the supply of raw material for processing and thus permit considerably more production. He next went to Los Angeles and hired his company's first sales manager, Ernest L. "Ernie" Stafford, who was already employed in a similar capacity at the company's local broker. This was an excellent choice for Charbonneau's challenging expansion campaign. A whiz-bang salesman, Stafford had long experience in the grocery store business, including the Safeway chain in Phoenix and Tucson. He had also worked in advertising and sales management for a Los Angeles coffee, tea, and spices manufacturer whose marketing territory covered five western states. Stafford already knew the Tree Top products line, and realized that additional advertising was essential as the next step.[8]

Bill Charbonneau shared in this opinion. He believed implicitly in the power of advertising and was ready to spend large sums on it. The Seattle consulting firm chosen for this assignment pointed out the main difficulty in such a promotional campaign. Because orange juice was the national favorite, it was first necessary to promote apple

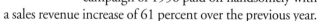

Label change from the original New West Tree Top (1947) to Charbonneau Tree Top in 1951.

juice itself as a desirable beverage, and then to tout the "brand personality" and virtues of Tree Top among its apple beverage competitors. And since there was no outstanding name and little advertising involving that fruit drink, it would be relatively easy to make Tree Top number one in the field. The best way to do so, as determined by research, was through television commercials aimed at mothers and children in afternoon shows.

Charbonneau focused most of his advertising budget for 1956 on three markets, Seattle, Los Angeles, and Arizona. Twenty-second animated commercials appealing to children focused on the Tree Top brand name with jingles such as "We pick, pick, the pick of the crop from the top, top, top of the tree." To sway mothers, the messages emphasized health benefits and taste appeal, and that the best apple juice must logically come from where the best, most famous apples grew—obviously Washington state. Some of the visual images were furnished by the Washington State Apple Commission, a notable instance of cooperation since that agency did not always sympathize with Tree Top's later activities. The initial television ad campaign of 1956 paid off handsomely with a sales revenue increase of 61 percent over the previous year.

Such impressive success called for more television advertising, particularly in 1958 to the spring of 1960, when the targeted places included Seattle, Tacoma, Los Angeles, Sacramento, San Diego, Phoenix, Tucson, and Billings. For example, using the same programs and format introduced in 1956, the firm ran 85 ads from late September to early December 1959 on three Los Angeles television stations. The commercials concentrated on such afternoon kids' shows as *Popeye*, *Sheriff John*, *Bozo the Clown*, and *Brakeman Bill's Cartoon Express*. Special commercials featuring apple cider ran for two weeks before Halloween. Charbonneau reveled in the dividends of television exposure. If his annual net income happened to be $500,000, he might immediately start planning to spend half of it on advertising for the coming year, despite warnings about the continual problem of raw product needed to match the ad campaign.[9]

Animated TV film spot, 1956–60.

In 1959, "Brakeman Bill" on KTNT-TV, Seattle-Tacoma, promotes Tree Top cider during the Halloween season.

It was this reality of supply, supply, supply that determined a major transition for the company. Charbonneau concluded that any large increase in tonnage of the raw

product must come from around Wenatchee. Consequently, he began planning to build a new processing plant there on 12 acres he already owned adjoining the railroad. It was another example of vintage Charbonneau hubris. When Wenatchee officials caused red-tape delays, he indignantly told them off and bought land on the edge of nearby Cashmere for his facility, which was completed in late 1959. This property had no direct access to rail transportation, but Charbonneau disliked railroads anyway and avoided using them for shipments whenever possible. The main trouble, however, was that for three years Tree Top could not get enough processor apples to meet the product demand created by its highly successful advertising program.

"Mayor Carl" on KRON-TV, San Francisco, 1959.

Charbonneau's managerial style during the 16 years before he sold out to the Tree Top cooperative was free-wheeling and unhindered by stockholders or a board of directors. It was his company, and he ran it as he pleased—a situation that explains many curious as well as humorous incidents. A firm believer in efficiency, Charbonneau commanded a tight operation with a lean staff. His office was in the plant building. For the most part, his regular office force only consisted of a stenographer, a bookkeeper, and Louie Hauser, in charge of billing and shipping. Sales manager Ernie Stafford and field agent Garfield C. "Gar" Barnett were in and out of the office. That was about it for the Charbonneau company's executive headquarters.

Louie Hauser was on the job five or six weeks before he actually met the boss, and then only in a brief encounter. In the same vein there were no staff meetings, and if Charbonneau wanted to discuss salaries or another matter, he would summon the individual out to his big Lincoln Continental for a parking lot conference, or perhaps drive around for awhile, and then buy the person a cup of coffee. To keep employees on their toes, he might deliberately make a mistake and see if they caught it. It was not unusual, however, for him to reward loyal workers at the end of a successful season by taking a large group of them on special excursions, such as a deep-sea fishing trip.

Although floor managers kept the plant operations running, Charbonneau spent much of his time checking on production activities. Abrupt and impulsive, he might "jump down the throat" of a worker or fire someone on the spot without much of an explanation. Ernie Stafford frequently had heated arguments with him, usually about ways to increase production, because of the sales manager's compulsion to sell more apple juice than was ever available. Not surprisingly, Charbonneau disliked the Teamsters union, which at some point had gained a foothold in his domain. He firmly believed that unions, besides undermining an owner's authority, took a big bite out of an employee's salary with little in return. Since he offered relatively high wages, good benefits, and, selectively at his discretion, substantial annual bonuses, Charbonneau considered a vote for the union as a sign of personal disloyalty to him.

This brand of fierce pride also extended to the marketplace. For years Charbonneau refused to cooperate with distributors who wanted their own separate, or "private," labels displayed on products manufactured by Charbonneau. When a national grocery chain giant demanded an individual label, threatening to remove Tree Top apple juice from its shelves all over Portland, he resolutely refused to back down, and suffered the consequences. It took real "guts" to make such a decision, knowing that it would result in the loss of substantial sales. But Charbonneau, the driven perfectionist, apparently viewed his proprietary stand on the label issue as part of his determination to personally guarantee the purity and taste of anything connected, even indirectly, to his name. After a few years, reportedly because of customer demand, the grocery chain started stocking the Tree Top brand again.

Undoubtedly, Charbonneau had his eccentricities, but he took a clearheaded, practical approach to solving the crucial problem of a reliable supply of apples. At that time, the supply pipeline started with the growers, who might consign their fruit to a broker, but they usually brought it to a warehouse, which, after sorting and grading, sold most of it to fresh-apple vendors, leaving the leftovers to the processors for juicing or drying. Charbonneau felt that he and the growers had a common adversary in the warehouse operators, who, as he saw it, had often treated him unfairly and charged the orchardists excessive fees. He planned to bypass the warehouses and go straight to the orchardists with a deal they could not refuse. He would sell his processing company to an organization of growers commonly called a cooperative, and they would own and operate it, as well as agree to provide an adequate supply of raw product. This idea was the genesis of the Tree Top Inc. cooperative.

As already shown, Charbonneau was a man of strong feelings, who expressed his views openly and in the most explicit terms. The formation of agricultural cooperatives had a long tradition in the United States, becoming especially prominent during the Populist Movement of the 1890s when farmers felt threatened by "monopoly capital." In Washington, fresh-apple growers had organized successful cooperatives that opened lucrative national and international markets.[10] In Charbonneau's case, however, he disliked the term "cooperative," much less the traditional meaning of the concept, believing that it suggested ties with socialism and thereby endorsed mediocrity as a substitute for the superior qualities of private corporate ownership. He developed a preference instead for the creative term "togetherness," which simply envisioned bringing together hundreds of growers in a common cause. Paul Fountain and Robert F. Brachtenbach, respectively Charbonneau's tax advisor and lawyer, soon learned to steer clear of any reference to a "cooperative." In fact, they probably suggested the idea of "togetherness," creating the term.

Charbonneau's decision to sell his prospering company was not made in a hurry, nor without legal advice. And, a family tragedy helped him make up his mind. He had made long-term plans for his older son, "Bill Jr." (William H. Charbonneau III), to take over the apple processing company, and for his younger son, Donald, to assume management of the family's orchard in the Yakima Valley. In 1953, Bill Jr. died in a mid-air plane collision while

William H. "Bill" Charbonneau
Founder of Tree Top Inc.

Bill Charbonneau founded what became Tree Top as a private company in 1944, and then sold his holdings for formation of a cooperative in 1960. His decision to make "Tree Top" his main brand name in 1947, and later adding an attractive logo, tells a great deal about the man himself. First, the paper label he was using lacked an eye-catching appeal, so he paid a large amount developing a bright, attractive foil strip instead. Next, he needed an equally compelling brand name. According to a common belief of that time, the choicest fruit grew at the top of trees, which may have influenced Charbonneau's decision. Supposedly, he already had "Tree Top" in mind, but delayed the announcement until after conducting a "Name the Brand" contest among plant workers and the five brokers representing the company. Only "Top Harvest" emerged in the poll to challenge Charbonneau's obvious favorite, so he registered the competing trademark for possible use later, and proclaimed "Tree Top" the winner.

Regarding the logo, one story claims that he paid a graphic artist $25,000 to do the job. When he showed the results to his wife, and they had discussed the mat-

ter at the kitchen table, Charbonneau leaned back and declared, "You know, for $25,000 some high school kid could do better than that." He scrapped the artist's work, and with his wife's help, devised the soon familiar logo of bright red apples on a green, leafy background, which began appearing on Tree Top bottles in 1953.

Probably there is some truth in both of these stories. After the formation of Tree Top, Charbonneau stayed on as general manager, until the board of directors arranged a financial settlement and dismissed him in 1965. He reluctantly severed his ties with the fruit processing operations he had created when he accepted the final payment at a Yakima bank. From the bank, he went to Tree Top headquarters in Selah and picked up his things.

In retirement, he continued to eat lunch daily at the Chinook Hotel in Yakima, invested in the stock market, and, ironically, considering his disdain for artificially sweetened "belly wash" beverages, traded in sugar futures. He also bought another 100 acres of orchard land in addition to the 100 acres of trees he already owned.

Bill Charbonneau never set foot on the Tree Top premises again.

serving in the U.S. Air Force. The father was devastated by this loss and never completely recovered emotionally. Without the designated "heir apparent" to step into his shoes, Charbonneau was inclined to look for other options. In one way or another, however, it always came back to the supply pipeline difficulty. Long a keen observer of the orange juice business, he had made a trip to Florida in the late 1950s for a firsthand investigation and consultation with leaders in that industry. He returned with the conviction that, like the Florida citrus processors, the only way to assure a reliable supply of apples was to involve the growers in the overall operation. And the only way to do that was to guarantee them a specific price for their fruit and pay the money up front. At that time, a cash advance in apple processing was unheard of—growers usually had to wait several months to get their money. Charbonneau had even more revolutionary proposals up his sleeve, as he would soon reveal.

First, it was necessary to formulate the legal framework. For that complicated task Charbonneau employed the young Selah lawyer, Robert F. Brachtenbach, who would later serve as a state representative and chief justice of the Washington state supreme court.[11] Charbonneau became convinced that the success of the new venture depended on his remaining as its manager, and Brachtenbach included in the final contract an ironclad clause to that effect, which withstood several court challenges to break it. Partially to satisfy Charbonneau's disdain for the concept, and even the word "cooperative," Brachtenbach did some creative legal footwork, which appeared in the new firm's articles of incorporation. He structured Tree Top ostensibly as a private corporation, but, in the provisions involving future stockholders, also as a potential public cooperative.

Not surprisingly, there were some attractive tax advantages for a corporation that also operated as a cooperative. These possibilities were certainly not overlooked, since the

Olofson accounting firm, where Charbonneau's financial adviser Paul Fountain was a member, had thoroughly researched this beforehand. Thus the firm became Tree Top Inc., which would lead to endless questions over the years about why a grower-owned agricultural cooperative would have "Inc." tacked onto its name like it was a Wall Street corporation. As it turned out, the provision that guaranteed Charbonneau's continuation as manager would draw the most attention. In fact, this provision would later lead to such intense friction between Charbonneau and the cooperative's board of directors that, amid recriminations, he was, in effect, fired from the firm he originally created.

In the "tentative plan" Charbonneau presented in the spring of 1960, he elaborated on his proposal to sell out to the growers. Instead of emphasizing the perennial shortfall of apples for processing, he took just the opposite tact, declaring that the current year would see "unmanageable surpluses," which would only increase in succeeding years. The logical solution for this unusual "problem," he said, was to see it coming and get "a fresh new horse to help carry Washington apples to market and one that the grower can ride to the bank with a feeling of confidence." In brief, Charbonneau's main pitch stressed the role of the suppliers and how they would reap the lion's share of the profits in the new venture.

More specifically, the Charbonneau Packing Corporation would transfer all its stock to a new firm called Tree Top Inc. for a price of $1,732, 000, to be paid over a 10-year period or less. The sum of $126,000 in "equipment contracts (2 year term)" had been deducted from a grand total of $1,858,000. In a breakdown of the selling price, accounts receivable and product inventories came to $473,000, and the Selah property and machinery amounted to another $545,000. For the Cashmere plant, only the machinery was included at $290,000, although Tree Top would hold an option to purchase the building and property.

A category entitled "Intangibles, goodwill, trademarks, etc.," was valued at $550,000. This item drew a great deal of comment. In the first place, it was said, the abrasive Charbonneau had no good will, and secondly, the Tree Top brand name was not worth that much. In the latter case, the critics were dead wrong because the Tree Top trademark alone proved to be worth far more than a half million dollars, supposedly the total amount Charbonneau claimed

he had spent on advertising in recent years. "If we'd had to start from scratch," said an astute insider with the cooperative, "we'd never have made it."[12]

Then came the clinchers in the whole deal. No interest would be charged on the sale price for the first five years, and thereafter a rate of 5 percent. Funds to pay off the debt would be obtained through binding 10-year contracts with the growers, who would agree to furnish apples to Tree Top for a guaranteed minimum price of $20 a ton. This promised minimum seemed like "pie in the sky" to skeptics since culls had seldom, if ever, brought more than $5 a ton in the past. Whether the tonnage price was $20 or more in a given year, however, $5 per ton of the amount would be reserved to pay off the debt to Charbonneau. When Charbonneau was paid in full, the suppliers might eventually receive a refund of the yearly $5 per ton deductions, recorded for each of them as individual purchases of capital stock. It was a brilliant plan, mainly because the grower-owners of the cooperative, without any financial liability to themselves, could go into business with virtually no down payment and a built-in way to liquidate the balance.

Charbonneau would hold mortgages on the property and machinery, but probably his main financial security resulted from the requirement that Tree Top employ him as manager for the 10-year period it owed him money, or for less time if he was paid off. His rather handsome salary at the time was $24,000 per year. Under the ironclad provision fashioned by lawyer Robert Brachtenbach, Charbonneau would have "full management" of Tree Top operations, with its policies determined by him, including marketing, production, personnel, and most of the advertising. On one hand, Charbonneau's almost complete control could be viewed as pure self-gratification. But it could also be seen as protection of the sizable debt owed to him by the cooperative. Regardless, the 12-member board of directors, made up of 6 growers from the Wenatchee area and 6 from around Yakima, was left with only routine duties. In fact, since Charbonneau regarded the directors as little more than figureheads, he was on a collision course with them from the start.

Incredibly, Charbonneau had to sell the growers on the good deal he was giving them. Even though he considered his proposal as "an idealistic approach" and in the orchardists' best interest, he was forced to conduct an arduous campaign to convince those same suppliers to sign up in contracts undergirding the whole grand scheme. In a series of meetings, usually held in Grange halls, up north in the Wenatchee area and down south in the Yakima Valley, he made the case for "togetherness" to the frequently unsympathetic listeners. All too often he heard them say, "Fine, but it won't work." Actually a talented group of his associates, including Brachtenbach and Fountain, made the pitch, while, because of Charbonneau's volatile nature, he remained seated in the front row of the audience.

In one incident at the Nob Hill Grange near Yakima, Charbonneau's associates were at the front making the presentation with charts and graphs when a grower at the back of the room stood up and raised his concerns about the risks involved. From his front-row seat in the audience, Charbonneau jumped up and heatedly responded, in effect, that his proposal would save growers from exactly those risks. It was at such gatherings up and down the state that north-south sectional differences became apparent. Strangely enough, Charbonneau's single-minded proposal brought two different reactions. To the north in the Wenatchee area and the Okanogan country, the audiences were more favorably disposed to his "togetherness" ideal because the growers there had more experience with cooperatives, and therefore placed more trust in the concept and its objectives. Down south around the Yakima Valley, orchardists more likely valued their independence and regarded cooperatives as having a socialistic connotation. And these two apple-growing sections had not only a sense of competition, but also suspicions about each other, a situation that would surface occasionally in the future causing difficulty for Tree Top.

The first 12-member board of directors organized Tree Top as a Washington corporation on May 10, 1960, and, two days later, the articles of incorporation were approved by the state supervisor of corporations. On July 1, 1960, the Charbonneau Packing Corporation ceased to exist and Tree Top Inc. took its place, even though the grower response, as measured by the tonnage of apples pledged to the new firm, had been less than enthusiastic. Charbonneau had specified that the contracts must guarantee 30,000 tons for processing before the transaction took place, but sign-ups had materialized for only 20,000 tons. He chose to overlook this shortcoming. With this point in mind, the question naturally arises as to Charbonneau's basic motives in the "togetherness" project.

On one hand, as he claimed, he was idealistic and generously charitable on behalf of the orchardists. Or, he might have used the growers to stabilize the supply pipeline, at least partially for his own sake since he became the general manager, or CEO, of the new firm. About this time he reportedly had received at least two offers from privately owned concerns to buy him out with cash on the barrelhead and at higher amounts than the Tree Top purchase price. Supposedly, Charbonneau had turned down these offers because, as a part of his legacy, he wanted to leave his processing operations in the hands of those who deserved them most; that is, the growers. Significantly, rumors also circulated that he was worried about a personal health problem, which might help explain his concern with such idealistic values. Whatever the case, it seems altogether possible that this shrewd businessman did have a genuine soft spot in his heart for the orchardists, or at least he looked with more favor on them than on the warehouse operators or other prospective buyers. 🍎

Endnotes

1. Possibly, Charbonneau had some connection with a fruit juice firm, Sun Valley Products Company, in Southern California before he moved to Portland. See the *Selah Valley Optimist*, October 12, 1944, which states as much at the time Charbonneau bought Pomona Products, the foundation for the Tree Top cooperative.

2. For early apple growing in the Pacific Northwest, see Amanda L. Van Lanen, "'We Have Grown Fine Fruit Whether We Would or No': The History of the Washington State Apple Industry, 1880–1930," Ph.D. dissertation, Washington State University, 2009, especially chapters 1 and 2.

3. James W. Scott, *Washington: A Centennial Atlas* (Bellingham: Center for Pacific Northwest Studies, Western Washington University, 1989), 2–12, 54–55.

4. *Selah Valley Optimist*, July 9, 1936, March 18, July 27, 1937, October 12, 1944. In the 1930s, Selah's "Fruit Row" consisted of eight or nine sizable warehouses and packing operations. Robert S. Lince, *The Selah Story: History of Selah, East Selah, and Wenas Valley in Yakima County, Washington* (Selah: Selah Valley Optimist Printing, 1984), 189, 196, 214. The Pomona company apparently was named for the Roman goddess of orchards and gardens.

5. For an example of Neubert's research, see Alfred Max Neubert, "A Study of the Effect of Filtration, Clarification, and Concentration on the Composition and Properties of Apple Juice," Ph.D. dissertation, State College of Washington, 1941.

6. *Selah Valley Optimist*, July 9, 1936. Another account states that Dr. Edvin Schoop, "a Swiss chemist" experienced in apple juice production, had brought specialized equipment from Switzerland that helped the original Pomona firm get started. Lince, *Selah Story*, 189. Still another source says that Cliff Ross brought a German expatriate living in Switzerland, a "Dr. Swoop" (probably

Schoop), to Selah where the European perfected his development of clear apple juice. *The Goodfruit Grower*, April 1, 2009.

7. Van Lanen, "We Have Grown Fine Fruit," chapter 3, discusses the difficulties experienced by orchardists in overcoming natural hazards.

8. Early advertising and promotional campaigns by the Washington apple industry are discussed in Van Lanen, "We Have Grown Fine Fruit," chapter 5.

9. More than 40 years later, in 2000, Tree Top was using the same approach in television advertising by sponsoring kids' shows, such as *Zaboomafoo*, *Barney*, and *Clifford and the Big Red Dog*, on PBS stations in Seattle and Portland. Peggy McDonald, vice president of marketing, emphasized that children under six years of age still drank the most apple juice, and added that mothers, who did the grocery shopping, watched these shows with their offspring. Thus the 10-second ads hit "both targets" with the catchy voice-overs of a kid seeing a glass slowly fill up with two red apples, and saying, "Tree Top Apple Juice…with the juice of two Washington apples in every glass." *Apple Corps*, November 2000; a Tree Top newsletter sent to employees.

10. Van Lanen, "We Have Grown Fine Fruit," 138–59; Tony Zaragoza, "Apple Capital: Growers, Labor, and Technology in the Origin and Development of the Washington State Apple Industry, 1890–1930," Ph.D. dissertation, Washington State University, 2007, chapter 3.

11. Ross Courtney, "Former State Supreme Court Justice Brachtenbach Dies," *Yakima Herald-Republic*, May 3, 2008.

12. Victor Morgan, an early "president" (chair) of the board of directors, interviewed in the *Omak Chronicle*, February 6, 1975.

Chapter 2

The Board of Directors in Control

The changeover from private ownership to a cooperative had little effect on Charbonneau's managerial style. The 12-member board of directors—who, incidentally, had each bought $100 of stock, or a total of $1,200, for the only actual capitalization of Tree Top Inc.—may have been handpicked by Charbonneau. Regardless, he considered them as mere stage props, usually going ahead with what he wanted to do and informing them about it later. As one indication of his approach, he authorized mileage compensation for their attendance at board meetings, but dragged his feet on per diem payments.

One of his newly proposed ventures, however, did raise some hackles, and led to serious trouble for him. Always keeping up with the successes of the citrus industry in Florida and California, Charbonneau decided that a comparable frozen concentrate of apple juice was the next major step for Tree Top. He was undoubtedly influenced by the research and advice of U.S. Department of Agriculture scientists, including that of Dr. Alfred M. Neubert, who had consulted with him at the startup of his privately owned firm. Several years before, Neubert had written about the encouraging commercial prospects for apple concentrate. Also, the method of producing concentrate that Charbonneau eventually used had been developed 10 years before by USDA research specialists, but employed commercially only on a small scale.[1]

Charbonneau's plans not only offered an innovative marketing idea, but also a way to save on transportation costs from the "far-corner" Pacific Northwest to other parts of the country. Otherwise, as a more direct benefit to the cooperative's grower-owners, Charbonneau was convinced that, while regular apple juice might have an average return of $45 per ton of raw product, the concentrate would average $75 a ton. In fact, Charbonneau had probably built the Cashmere plant with the ambitious objective of using its concentrate production as a means of "going nationwide" in head-on competitive marketing with the citrus industry.

Although the board adopted his proposal, some members, described as "fresh apple men," remained suspicious of such a bold, expensive departure from established methods of processing. To the opponents, Charbonneau had just talked them into long-term contracts to make old-time juice, and now he wanted to do something completely different. One board member threw up his hands in disgust and resigned on the spot when the vote was taken. Others consulted a lawyer about challenging Charbonneau's 10-year management agreement in court but learned it was ironclad. This kind of heated opposition placed Charbonneau, the driven perfectionist with high standards for authentic taste, in a difficult position, but he rammed the proposition through anyway. More stress arose in obtaining the funds to purchase the venture's expensive new machinery. Two loan applications by the cooperative failed, and Charbonneau had to use his own credit connections with a Seattle bank to borrow $350,000 plus $150,000 more, if needed. Nevertheless, in late 1963, Tree Top became the first processing concern to produce and market frozen concentrated apple juice on a large scale. It was an almost immediate success in both consumer acceptance and profits.

Charbonneau's stubborn efforts against an undercurrent of opposition had some far-reaching implications. With the help of government scientists and private manufacturers, he had introduced in Washington a new production system for apple processing and the equipment to do the job. The main objective, of course, involved distilling off the apple's "essence" from the juice. Then, under low heat and high vacuum pressure to avoid scorching, three-quarters of the water was extracted. Next, the essence was returned to the concentrated juice, mixed and packed in cans, and frozen. Since the basic substance deteriorated rapidly, the tricky part came in replacing it in the concentrate without losing its fresh-fruit taste and smell.

After months of feverish work by Charbonneau and his consultants, the project delivered several cases of brightly

Tree Top's First Board of Directors

Three members of the first Board of Directors: (l. to r.) Orville Ormiston of Yakima, Hubert W. "Hugh" Burnett of Chelan, and A.T. "Thor" Fossum of Yakima.

According to the Tree Top's bylaws, the board of directors must have six members from the Northern District (Wenatchee/Okanogan area) and six from the Southern District (Yakima/Columbia Basin/Oregon and Idaho). Today, Interstate Highway 90, which crosses the Columbia River at Vantage, Washington, is roughly the dividing line, although where growers deliver their fruit for processing determines the tonnages credited to each district.

Tree Top was incorporated under the laws of the State of Washington on May 10, 1960. The first board members representing their fellow growers were Hubert W. "Hugh" Burnett of Chelan, Grant M. Call of Tonasket, Roy E. Coulthard of Cashmere, A.T. "Thor" Fossum of Yakima, Robert Hartley of Manson, Victor Morgan

of Omak, Orville Ormiston of Yakima, Otis Riggs of Wapato, Desmond Shearer of Tieton, Charles B. Stoll of Yakima, Ralph Strand of Cowiche, and James Welch Jr. of East Wenatchee.

These original, incorporating directors must have been "true believers" in the cooperative concept, as shown by the fact they received no pay for their services and no reimbursement for expenses. They donated their own time and paid their own way. Moreover, they all had paid $100 for the "privilege" of membership. That is, besides a substantial bank loan, the purchase by individual directors of 100 shares of common stock at $1 each, or a total of $1,200, was the only capital investment originally recorded for the incorporation of Tree Top. It took several years before adjustments were made to adequately compensate and reimburse board members.

Charles B. Stoll served briefly as the first board president (later changed to chairman), followed by Orville Ormiston. Then Victor Morgan, who was a board member for 13 years, headed the group for a record 5 years (1963–68). In 1975, Morgan looked back and reflected that many had thought the formation of a processing cooperative was a foolish idea. But, he declared, "Tree Top is here to stay," and also observed with satisfaction, "The greatest thing Tree Top did was to help keep the market for apples steady."[1] In short, after only 15 years, the efforts of the first board of directors had resulted in the creation of a real market for lowly culls, which had helped provide a firm foundation under the entire apple industry's price structure.

---

1. Morgan, interview in the *Omak Chronicle*, February 6, 1975.

---

colored, six-ounce cans of concentrate frozen at zero degrees.[2] He had proudly served samples of the reconstituted juice at the 1963 annual board meeting, declaring triumphantly in a prediction that would prove substantially true: "Production and sale of concentrated apple juice by Tree Top could possibly repeat the Florida orange juice story and result in doubling orchard prices." Then, when other loan applications failed, he had underwritten the financing of the new endeavor, obtained the necessary

equipment, and closely supervised the installation and first production. It was a virtuoso performance of lasting significance. By 1971, Tree Top concentrated apple juice was being marketed across 80 percent of the country with 50 percent of the national population. Besides lower shipping costs than for the bulkier regular, or single strength, juice, an obvious advantage of concentrate was its longer storage life, which could help ensure continued processing in short crop years.

In the end, however, Charbonneau's historic achievement for the apple industry, although bringing him recognition and great personal satisfaction, was a costly victory. The bruised egos and resentment resulting from this battle became a contributing factor when the board eventually rose up and voted to dismiss him as general manager. Even when Charbonneau was obviously on the right track, as in the case of frozen concentrate, it was still difficult for some people to agree with him.

Meanwhile, sales manager Ernie Stafford, in tandem with Tree Top's Seattle promotional agency, prepared to devote all of his attention to an advertising-distribution program for the new product in three market areas: Spokane, Seattle, and Southern California. Again animated cartoons were used on kids' afternoon television shows, and a series of spot commercials ran on radio stations. Full-page, two-color newspaper ads for the frozen concentrated drink gave a slightly different meaning to Charbonneau's concern for authentic taste by featuring the slogan, "You've Never Tasted Fresh Apple Juice Before." Encouraged by consumer acceptance and impressive sales in the initial markets, Stafford set out to add more outlets for the concentrate. Like a western whirlwind, he swept across the countryside, opening markets in northern California and Arizona, then into new trade territory in the Southwest at Dallas and Houston, and on into the Midwest, the South, and the remaining 11 western states. One novel way of convincing wholesale buyers was to give them a "healthy swig" of the chilled juice brought along in special thermos bottles. Only in Chicago did Stafford's sales campaign bog down, primarily because that market area was controlled

You've Never Tasted Fresh Apple Juice Before 🍎!

TREE TOP PURE FROZEN APPLE JUICE

Now You Can!

Fresh Frozen Washington Apple Juice Comes To Texas!

CLIP & SAVE! Redeemable at your grocer's

SAVE 10¢ ON THE PURCHASE of TWO 6-oz. CANS or ONE 12-oz. CAN of TREE TOP PURE FROZEN APPLE JUICE

STORE COUPON

by just a few chain groceries and one distributor, making it difficult for newcomers to get a start.

By 1964, Tree Top had improved the supply pipeline of raw product until it was getting nearly one-quarter of all the fruit available for processors in Washington. If Charbonneau had not inaugurated the production of frozen concentrated juice, and equipped the Cashmere plant to do the job, the cooperative could not have handled that volume, and probably some of the year's bumper crop of apples would simply have been dumped. Grower-members who had contracted with Tree Top received $40 per ton, and Charbonneau confidently predicted that they would see the day of $100 a ton, which many dismissed as "crazy." Within a decade or so, however, the total grower return would hit a tonnage rate ranging from $145 to $160, depending on the apple varieties involved, although this figure tended to fluctuate and did not remain that high permanently.

Tensions between Charbonneau and the Tree Top board of directors grew steadily. Sensing the widening gulf, Charbonneau started sending each director a monthly newsletter in which he emphasized Tree Top's successful, and therefore profitable, marketing campaigns. Even though the cooperative had kept its prices up at a "respectable" level, it had beat out its legitimate competition from lower-priced brands as well as the phony sales pitches of the watered-down, "belly-wash" beverages. He also made a point of stressing the favorable reception, so far, for the concentrate and the rosy prospects for it in the future. Implying that frozen apple juice might well match the success of the Florida citrus industry, Charbonneau emphasized that

Max Steward, the Fossum Brothers, and Gar Barnett and the Founding of Tree Top

Max Steward.

It would be hard to describe a typical member of Tree Top, but Max Steward's part in the formation of the cooperative and his long career in the orchard business as a small, independent grower make an appealing story. At age 21 and exempt from the World War II draft, Steward left Kansas and moved to the Yakima area in 1943. Three years later he bought a 30-acre orchard up the Naches Valley at Gleed. For the next 55 years he worked his acreage, hiring pickers and some other help for such chores as pruning, but mostly depending on his own labor. Thirty acres were enough for him; he never wanted more.

Steward's crops were never completely frozen out, although there was one unusually bad hail storm as well as occasional damaging sleet that took a toll. The price of fruit and making a living, not the weather, were always his main concern. Although Steward actually lost money in only two seasons, he did take a part-time job for a few years in Yakima at a brother's television store, while his orchard was "renewing" itself. He worked his acreage during the morning for about five hours, and left at noon for the job, often staying there for another eight hours. When replanting the orchard, he chose Red Delicious, Golden Delicious, Winesap, and Long Red Rome apple varieties, and also put in pears when they became profitable. Incredibly, Steward never owned a truck or a pickup, but hauled all his own fruit to the warehouse in 30- and 50-gallon barrels in the back of his car.

In his limited spare time, Max Steward took an active role in the local horticultural club. As vice president of the Naches Valley organization, he was closely associated with Garfield C. "Gar" Barnett, the president, and Martin Fossum, the program chair, and several other members of that body who became instrumental in the founding of the Tree Top cooperative. During the spring of 1960, Bill Charbonneau was busily promoting the sale of his private company for the creation of Tree Top. His main venues for approaching the fruit growers were at meetings in Grange halls throughout the Yakima and Wenatchee areas. Skepticism about Charbonneau's proposition was particularly strong in the Yakima district, and support of the Naches Valley organization played a crucial part in overcoming this negative sentiment. In fact, Gar Barnett, who was highly regarded among

orchardists in the Yakima area, had worked for Charbonneau, at least part-time, as a field representative, and had a good understanding of what was at stake. His influence may well have helped turn the tide.

Max Steward became a member of the Tree Top cooperative and usually attended the annual meetings, but his 30 acres of fruit trees took most of his time. Gar Barnett had an important role in Tree Top's formative years, serving as field manager among growers in the Southern District. He was especially effective in persuading Oregon and Idaho orchardists to become members of the cooperative. An enthusiastic booster of the apple industry, Barnett literally "'died with his field boots on'" when he collapsed and died shortly after giving a spirited talk at a growers' meeting in Boise in November 1973. After he helped launch the cooperative, Martin Fossum left the fruit-growing business. However, his brother, A.T. "Thor" Fossum, who had also backed Charbonneau's plan, became an original incorporator of Tree Top and a member of the first board of directors.

During his 25 years on the board, Thor Fossum received several awards and honors for his distinguished record in the Washington fruit industry. Probably the highlight of his long service occurred in 1984 when Dr. Randall E. Torgerson, head of the Agricultural Cooperative Service, U.S. Department of Agriculture, came from Washington, D.C., to address the Tree Top annual meeting. Before his talk, Torgerson presented the prestigious national Cooperative Statesmanship Award to Fossum and his wife, Irene. After the address, Fossum thanked Dr. Torgerson and "bonded" with him as he and the high federal official casually conversed in Norwegian.[1]

In 1985, with wife Irene standing at his side, A.T. "Thor" Fossum receives an award for 25 years of service with the Tree Top board of directors.

Tree Topics, December 1973, and October and November 1984.

the new venture would increase the income of Tree Top's grower-owners accordingly.

These informative communications did little to improve a rapidly deteriorating situation. For instance, the board became fully aware that when Charbonneau sold out to the cooperative, he had retained the limited right to display the Tree Top label when marketing fresh fruit, which he had done in some shipments from his own orchard. After a round of bargaining discussions, he signed over exclusive control of the trademark in September 1964. Probably, Charbonneau's health problems also contributed to the already tense situation by making a reconciliation of viewpoints more difficult. Driven and always under a nervous strain, he had been plagued by respiratory trouble.

That fall the board actually challenged Charbonneau for the first time. As pointed out earlier, he had underwritten the financing of Tree Top's operations through his own credit connections with a Seattle bank, in both the loan for frozen concentrate equipment and the day-to-day expenditures necessitating a cash flow. In short, he always had to weigh his personal involvement with this bank debt against the wages and other expenses of running two processing plants. Under these circumstances, he wanted to avoid the extra expenses of a big carryover inventory. So it seemed logical to Charbonneau to shut down a plant for a few months and save money. As it happened, the Selah facility had been running a two-shift schedule from October 1964 until April 1965, when the incoming supply of apples started decreasing, and Charbonneau closed its operations. Some contracted growers immediately protested, asking that the Selah plant remain open at least through mid-June to process the sizable tonnages of fruit they still had on hand from a bumper crop. Charbonneau refused these demands, on the basis that continued operations would create expenses exceeding the bank's credit limits. Taking the side of the growers, the board got the Seattle bank's permission to run on one shift as long as it could be justified by the supply of raw product. The directors had gone over Charbonneau's head, and there was nothing he could do about it.

Charbonneau was on his way out. The bare facts are easily outlined. In the summer of 1965, the board applied to the Spokane Bank for Cooperatives, a financial agency of the U.S. Department of Agriculture, for a loan to pay off the debt to Charbonneau and dismiss him as general manager, purchase the Cashmere plant and property for $256,000, retire the Seattle bank loans and other debts, and provide operating funds. To satisfy the Bank for Cooperatives, the growers had to make new 10-year contracts with pledges to deliver cull apples to Tree Top. A.E. Van Winkle, a bank vice president, told the directors that assurance of 30,000 tons of fruit would be necessary "for a reasonably successful" business operation, and as a form of equity. By that fall the growers had signed up for only 20,000 tons, but the bank management, eager to promote the overall apple industry through Tree Top's processing of lower grades of fruit, extended the credit anyway. After making the loan, the Bank for Cooperatives frequently assumed an influential role in the firm's management and general operations.

The detailed story involving personalities and individual as well as corporate objectives is much more complex. For the Tree Top directors, Charbonneau either had to change his managerial tactics and consult with them or they would make a change sending him "down the road kicking his hat." Since he would not—in fact, could not—alter his style, the only alternative was to buy him out. The 12 directors were experienced apple growers, but since Charbonneau had run a one-man operation, they had a limited knowledge of corporate management. When they met with officers of the Bank for Cooperatives in Spokane, no one seemed to know exactly how much money they needed. Finally, bank vice president Van Winkle took over and started writing down different amounts, adding $500,000 at the end to cover operating expenses for a year. At this point some of the faces around the table started showing signs of dismay as the directors realized what they were getting into. But they were determined to gain control of Tree Top's affairs, and this was the only way to do it.

Charbonneau knew that the directors were negotiating with the Spokane bank to buy him out and end his management contract, but he was probably surprised that they could pull it off. In fact, his doubts were well founded. With a total credit line of $3 million—a $1.5 million "facility loan" and another $1.5 million for operations—the bank officials took a far greater risk with Tree Top than any other commitment they had made. In this case it was an amazing 90 percent of the financing to a mere 10 percent based on assets.

The final payment to Charbonneau was a check for $1 million; smaller amounts had been paid to him earlier. With

Chronological Listing
Chairmen of the Board of Directors

The board's officers, elected every year by the board itself immediately after the annual meeting, consist of a chairman, vice chairman, and secretary-treasurer. The announcement of elections centered on the date of the annual meeting of the grower-members, which was changed from March to November in 1972; at that same time, the top position's title was changed from "president" to "chairman of the board."

Charles B. Stoll, 1960–61

Orville Ormiston, 1962–63

Victor Morgan, 1963–68

Wilbur Nelson, 1968–72

Hubert W. "Hugh" Burnett, 1972–74*

Orville Ormiston, 1974–76

Raymond O'Neal, 1976–78

A.T. "Thor" Fossum, 1978–80

Ray Colbert, 1980–82

Cragg Gilbert, 1982–84

Charles Peters, 1984–86

Peter Van Well, 1986–88

George Chapman, 1988–90

Roger Strand, 1990–92

John Clayton, 1992–94

John Borton, 1994–96

Tom Auvil, 1996–98

Ray Keller, 1998–2000

Doug Stockwell, 2000–02

Dick Olsen, 2002–04

Fred Valentine, 2004–06

Bruce Allen, 2006–08

Tom Auvil, 2008–10

*Burnett had the title of board "president" at the March 1972 annual meeting, but was reelected as "chairman" in November 1972.

the check in hand, a delegation of three board members—probably A.T. "Thor" Fossum, Victor Morgan, and Orville Ormiston—met Charbonneau in the lobby of a Yakima bank. It was November 24, 1965, the morning before Thanksgiving, and the members wanted to wind things up quickly so they could get away on holiday trips. Showing great reluctance to take this final step, Charbonneau delayed accepting the check, putting a little different twist on his trademark phrase, "I want my money." First, he said that the check was $100 short, until it was explained at length that the amount had been covered in a previous payment. Then, since it was not a certified check, he raised the question of whether Tree Top actually had such a large amount on deposit yet. A phone call to the Spokane Bank for Cooperatives, which provided firm assurances, solved that problem. And so, Charbonneau's painful ordeal continued, as he delayed as long as possible ending his association with the firm he had created and nurtured for 21 years. Finally, in the afternoon, Charbonneau took the check and left.

The Tree Top board severed its last ties with Charbonneau in a meeting on March 1, 1967, with a vote to remove his name from the firm's label and all of its products. But his influence remained. During Charbonneau's 21 years at the helm, starting in 1944 under his private ownership and from 1960 to 1965 as the cooperative's general manager, he had laid a solid foundation with his meticulous, hands-on management. As tangible signs of his handiwork, Charbonneau had left behind the widely known trademark name and logo, a successful advertising and marketing program, the promising frozen concentrate product, quality control systems at both the Selah and Cashmere plants, and most obviously, the basis for a dependable pipeline of raw product through contracted growers who supplied the processing facilities they owned. Of equal significance, Charbonneau had established rigid requirements for purity, quality, and authentic taste as Tree Top hallmarks. These standards alone were so ingrained in the firm's operations that they served as his legacy to the apple industry long after his departure and the removal of his name from labels and boxes. In effect, he had sketched out the roadmap to future levels of achievement. As long as Tree Top adhered to Charbonneau's basic principles, it flourished, and whenever it deviated, even accidentally, there could be difficulty.

Another part of Charbonneau's legacy aroused a determination by the directors that they would never again be dominated or misled by management. Future administrators must work in close harmony with the board and not start the development of new, untried products or programs without strong backing from the directors. Furthermore, it must be understood that the cooperative consisted of a triangular structure beginning with hundreds of growers, whose wishes were expressed through the board of directors, who refined and translated these desires for implementation to the executive, who must always keep in mind the best interests of the grower-owners. Significantly the board itself was composed of prominent orchardists elected from the general membership. As a result, Tree Top was more "democratic" or more responsible to its base than a strictly private corporation, with perhaps thousands or millions of remote stockholders and a detached board of directors, in which executive power had fewer limitations. Leadership in a cooperative was still necessary, but on a more restricted basis. In short, the Tree Top structure roughly resembled the government of the United States—a representative democracy or republic, with its strengths as well as weaknesses.[3]

For several years, then, the board kept a tight rein on its administrators, quickly restraining those who went astray. This wariness resulted in a series of general managers in a relatively short time, while the now-liberated directors got their feet on the ground and searched for stability. In fact, at the beginning the board met two or three times a month in long sessions and pretty much ran things themselves. Key members also made frequent trips to the Selah headquarters for on-the-spot decision making. It must be remembered that the directors, and the grower-members as well, were primarily involved in the fresh-apple trade, the main source of their income, and secondarily in the processor market. As immediately became apparent to the board members, they were "absolute babes in the woods" on taking complete charge of a processing firm. And it was not easy to find an executive with the qualifications to run the complex operations of an agricultural cooperative. When interviewed, a couple of prospective candidates inquired about Tree Top's long-term master plan, and got in reply a discourse on Charbonneau's high standards and vision.

It was Tree Top's financial sponsor, the Spokane Bank for Cooperatives, that came to the rescue. Bank officials always modestly asserted that they refrained from direct interference in Tree Top's affairs, but, with a sizable loan outstand-

ing, simply made suggestions so that the cooperative would have "acceptable management." Regardless of the terminology, the Bank for Cooperatives closely monitored Tree Top's financial operations and paid particular attention to the hiring of general managers. In fact, a bank vice president, A.E. Van Winkle, frequently attended meetings of the board. Thus, it was no surprise that the Spokane bank had recommended a specific interim administrator, and that Tree Top had quickly made arrangements to hire that same person, who was on the job five days after Charbonneau's departure.

Highly regarded by the Bank for Cooperatives, 70-year-old James E. Klahre, the retired manager of an apple growers' cooperative, Diamond Fruit Growers at Hood River, Oregon, had more than 25 years of experience in this field. His instructions from the bank were to find his own permanent replacement. As it turned out, Klahre's mellow personality and exceptional management skills were just what Tree Top needed in that first year or so after Charbonneau's control ended.

Since Charbonneau had run a one-man show, he had no chain-of-command structure, much less an organizational chart. Klahre followed the opposite path, frequently consulting staff personnel on various matters. In short order he drew up a document that described the functions and responsibilities of each managerial position, including those of the general manager. For good measure he also specified a role for the board of directors that gave them the final word on all important matters, while still leaving management a realm of leadership and decision-making. A prominent feature of this document was a set of criteria for evaluation of the general manager's performance. The share of available culls obtained and the net profits per ton of apples processed stood highest on the list. As for growth, Klahre called for an increase in sales by 15 percent annually for the next five years, based on an expected 30,000 tons of raw product in the 1965–66 season and comparably greater tonnages thereafter. During his brief tenure, Klahre also initiated long-range planning, an updated quality control system at the Selah and Cashmere plants, the submission of reports by department heads at board meetings, and a detailed operating budget process that estimated costs down to various container sizes.

Under "Jimmy" Klahre's leadership, a more collegial atmosphere emerged at Tree Top, which was reflected in

General Managers/Presidents/CEOs

William H. Charbonneau, 1960–65*

James E. Klahre, 1965–67**

B.C. "Bud" Robbins, 1967–68

Ernest L. Stafford, 1968–69**

Robert E. Ward, 1969–82

Dennis J. Colleran, 1982–89**

Robert S. Conroy, 1989–92**

Frank Elsener, 1992–99

Thomas P. Stokes, 1999–Present

---

*Starting with Charbonneau, the title was "general manager"; in 1972 Ward was made "president and general manager"; Colleran was the first "president and chief executive officer," and his successors have held the same title.

**Interim positions—In the case of Klahre, who served for an extended period, he was told to continue until his permanent replacement was named. Stafford filled in as general manager after the board asked for Robbins' resignation. Colleran served briefly as interim before his permanent appointment. The public announcement of retired corporate executive Conroy's hiring stated that he would hold the post only until a permanent leader was found, but his tenure lasted more than three years.

major policy and personnel changes. At the first annual meeting after Charbonneau left, held on March 15, 1966, it was announced that the cooperative would accept a new maximum amount of fruit from the most loyal growers; that is, those who signed "100% contracts." Klahre reported that whereas in 1959 the average price for processor apples had been about $22 per ton, Tree Top had paid an average of $39 a ton for the five-year period 1960–65. He also said that the cooperative's share of available processor apples had increased from 13.5 percent in 1960 to 23 percent in 1965. In what amounted to a vindication of Bill Charbonneau's fixation on concentrate, sales manager Ernie Stafford told the board that in those outlets where the frozen beverage was marketed, the sales of regular juice had not decreased, as some directors feared, but instead had increased.

Stafford's sales program was already a proven success, and needed only a little fine-tuning for opening new markets in

a logical progression, as the money became available. But the old problem of the supply pipeline remained. In deciding on additional credit for Tree Top's routine operations, the Spokane Bank for Cooperatives customarily estimated whether the number of grower contracts would provide the raw product required for expanded marketing. In January 1966, funds had been on hand to introduce frozen concentrated apple juice in Boise and Salt Lake City, followed by a remnant of the Texas market, El Paso, and then nearby Albuquerque, New Mexico. These last places completed a blanketing of the western states. For the rest of the year a follow-up promotional blitz would finish the job—as long as the money lasted. Stafford's notable success in sales and marketing was recognized in August 1966 when Klahre—significantly, with the board's conspicuous approval—gave him the added duties of assistant general manager.

As expected, the problem of an adequate supply of processor apples claimed Klahre's constant attention. In informative news bulletins, he described Tree Top's successful marketing program and called on unaffiliated growers to join the cooperative and share the profits. He also went on the speaking circuit, proclaiming his firm's accomplishments at trade association meetings and in public talks. An unexpected opportunity to increase the supply pipeline arose when Tree Top received an offer to buy out the Valley Evaporating Company at Cowiche, Washington, a fruit-drying operation, not a juice processor. It seemed like a good acquisition, both financially and for access to additional supplies of raw product.

The Tree Top directors approached the prospective property cautiously. A committee was appointed to study the proposal and obtain an appraisal of Valley Evap's net value. In the end, Klahre, who had investigated the company's production and marketing records, recommended against the purchase. The board put the proposal on hold for further consideration, and later voted it down. Like a rejected lover, Evap had to wait for a more opportune time to join Tree Top. But it was inevitable, or at least predictable, that someday the board would shed its reluctance and welcome such opportunities to expand.

Garfield C. "Gar" Barnett, who operated his own orchard in the Yakima area, had worked for Charbonneau's private firm and started with Tree Top on a part-time basis as a field representative in the Southern District. He was so highly respected and so well informed on fruit growing,

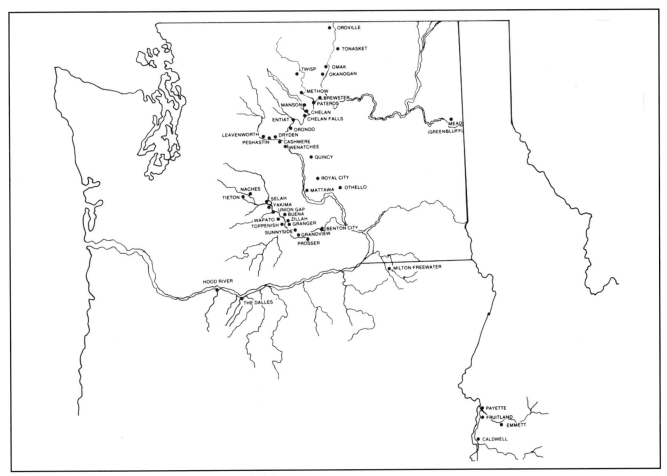

Grower membership areas in Washington, Oregon, and Idaho.
Tree Top Annual Report (October 1980).

however, that he was soon recruited for full-time employment. Barnett often traveled into Oregon and Idaho for his duties, and, in effect, opened up those states for Tree Top. Apple growing had flourished for many years both in Oregon, principally in the Hood River Valley, and in Idaho, mainly in the southwestern corner of the state around Payette.[4] Tree Top had started getting deliveries from Oregon in 1960, and orchardists there, under Barnett's guidance, subsequently gained membership in the cooperative. Likewise, a special session of the board of directors in July 1971 approved the same status for those Idaho growers who signed a 10-year contract. This agreement specifically excluded the Rome variety and stipulated that the shippers must pay all freight charges over $10 per ton.

The inclusion of Oregon and Idaho growers in the Tree Top membership was a routine business decision, not a grandstand play of territorial expansion. That is, these

orchardists might well provide significant additional tonnages of raw product, which the cooperative could use. The addition of out-of-state apples, however, did necessitate a change in those Tree Top labels bearing the caption "Made from Washington State Apples." The new version became "Blended with Washington State Apples."

On February 1, 1967, Jimmy Klahre had relinquished his management responsibilities to B.C. "Bud" Robbins, who had been the manager of a major Welch Grape Juice plant. Klahre apparently made the recommendation, and the Tree Top board as well as the Spokane Bank for Cooperatives readily approved it. Although Klahre had tutored Robbins on the requirements of the job, it soon became apparent that the two men had different management styles. Whereas Klahre thought things over at length before making a decision, especially if the answer was "No," Robbins was a man of action who often came to quick conclusions. Robbins wanted Tree Top to reach its full potential by taking bold steps in expansion without unnecessary delays. The cautious board of directors was not ready to approve such steps without a thorough investigation and measured deliberation. Dedicated to progress and creating an outstanding managerial record, Robbins was placed in a difficult situation during this post-Charbonneau period of adjustment. In the end, to put it simply, the directors thought Robbins was "going too far, too fast."

At first Robbins had the good luck of seeing a bumper crop of apples for 1967, with Tree Top getting all the raw product it wanted. The Cashmere plant produced so much frozen concentrate that extra warehouse space had to be obtained. With these encouraging signs, sales manager Ernie Stafford launched a new marketing program, starting with New Orleans and followed methodically by the rest of Louisiana and the three nearby states of Arkansas, Tennessee, and Alabama. Charles Parker, the cooperative's regional sales manager, and nine newly appointed brokers handled the details of opening these new outlets. At the same time, substantial radio advertising blanketed the already existing market areas, mainly the western states. Price increases covered these costs and promised additional income to the grower-owners.

Another indication of smooth sailing for Robbins was presented in a status report by James Miller, the Seattle advertising executive in charge of the cooperative's account. Addressing the firm's annual meeting in March 1968, Miller used convincing examples to assure his listeners that

Ernest L. Stafford (left) and B.C. "Bud" Robbins.
The Goodfruit Grower (December 1, 1967)

Tree Top had "the outstanding apple juice in the nation, the absolute leader in product quality." In the West, where its beverage had become the established leader, Tree Top's consistently high quality had forced competing brands to improve their standards. And nationally, Miller pointed out, consumers bought well over twice as much apple sauce as apple juice, but in the West, where Tree Top reigned, the purchasing record was reversed by a comfortable margin of 37 percent. More specifically, Los Angeles was the largest market area in the West, and the Washington cooperative had captured 40 percent of sales there, despite the competition of about 35 other brands. This impressive record in the West, Miller predicted, would soon be duplicated in other regional markets as the frozen concentrate became more widely distributed.

Early on, Robbins's persuasiveness helped overcome the reluctance of the board to launch major new projects. After difficult negotiations with its owners, Robbins had struck a deal for Tree Top to buy an existing apple dehydration concern, the Chelan Packing Company of Wenatchee. In this case, the Tree Top board of directors was not exactly blind-sided. The long, thorough consideration of purchasing the Valley Evaporating Company, although rejected, had revealed the advantages of diversification in processing beyond apple juice and frozen concentrate. The acquisition of an apple-drying or dehydration concern would provide another product line to bolster marketing campaigns. Then there was the potential benefit of stabilizing the erratic supply pipeline with the additional tonnage of other culls customarily accompanying the "peelers" used in dried-apple production. In fulfillment of the cooperative's mission, a dehydration plant like Chelan Packing would serve the best interests of the grower-members by offering them an additional outlet for their low-grade fruit.

With the convincing persuasion of Robbins, and after a lengthy discussion of the proposal, the board voted unanimously in June 1968 to buy Chelan Packing for $1,050,000. Probably the deciding factor was a favorable report submitted by trusted former general manager James E. Klahre. Later some directors concluded that it would have been better, and cheaper, to build and equip a totally new facility at Wenatchee. From the time Robbins hammered out the original deal with the former owners, the process of integrating the Wenatchee plant into Tree Top operations had its difficulties.

In a decision that appeared logical for transition purposes, the two owner-partners, William R. Dorsey and Sumner I. Strashun, were retained in managerial posts on two-year contracts. Under this arrangement, the Wenatchee plant, called the Chelan Packing Division, operated as a semi-autonomous part of Tree Top with separate accounting and management procedures. Some board members questioned this arrangement, recalling the tensions arising when Bill Charbonneau had stayed on as general manager after selling out to the cooperative.

The Tree Top board, still sensitive to any threat to its authority, became increasingly concerned about exactly what was going on at the new facility. This concern focused on two fronts. The Wenatchee plant had outmoded equipment that experienced frequent breakdowns and might go out completely at any time. In addition, the former owners, who stayed on, lacked a firsthand knowledge of how a cooperative worked and of Tree Top's particular guiding principles. The unusual arrangement continued until the board, in August 1969, fully integrated the Chelan Packing Company into the Tree Top structure and soon hired new management at Wenatchee. Dorsey and Strashun were assigned to other positions in different parts of the cooperative.

Earlier, the Wenatchee plant had helped give Tree Top an unexpected publicity boost when Quaker Oats started running color ads on national television for its new instant oatmeal with cinnamon and apple ingredients. Featuring the source of the ingredients, the ads depicted a Ceylon cinnamon grower and his family, and also showed the well-known, colorful Washington orchardist and Tree Top member, Grady Auvil of Orondo, and some of his family. The Auvils were pictured sampling the breakfast cereal, which contained dehydrated apple flakes from the Wenatchee installation. Although Tree Top itself was not mentioned by name in the commercials, those TV viewers familiar with the apple industry readily attributed the fruit ingredient to the Selah-based firm.

General Manager B.C. Robbins devoted a great deal of time and attention to the troubled plant at Wenatchee. In fact, some board members began to question whether he spent enough time at the Cashmere and Selah facilities. The Wenatchee unit probably was uppermost in his mind, but it was during Robbins's tenure that Tree Top's most important innovation of the decade started having an impact. Earlier, the directors had decided to placate the cooperative's apple-growing members who also raised pears. These orchardists could often find a market for only part of their pear crop, and the culls had to be discarded. Bill Charbonneau had dismissed any suggestion of processing this fruit, saying the only possible use for pear juice or concentrate was as part of a cocktail mix. At other times, he declared he was having enough trouble handling apples without taking on another fruit, or that the demand for pear juice was so small there was no hope for profit in it.

Only by great effort over several years had Tree Top managed to achieve the impressive goal of taking cull apples, also previously considered worthless and bound for the dump, and giving them a significant marketplace value. It seemed that the same long, arduous campaign would be required if low-grade pears ever enjoyed a similar status. When he was interim general manager, James E. Klahre had shown the first real signs of interest and authorized the Cashmere plant to begin a concentrate pilot project in 1967. Staff members immediately began designing the mechanical changes necessary for the production of pear concentrate. The full implications of this landmark experiment, initiated by Klahre, came home while Bud Robbins was general manager.

The directors apparently had endorsed this departure from Tree Top's customary production activities because of their confidence in Klahre, whose past experience in Oregon had included various types of fruit, and because it was only a relatively small pilot project. According to a company publication: "[The] Board of Directors approved this project on a development basis, recognizing that in big crop years the existing facilities could not be made available for any pear operations. However, big oaks from little acorns grow."[5] How true this old adage turned out to be! The first run of several hundred tons of D'Anjou and Bartlett pears, supplied by Wenatchee area packing houses, were processed into concentrate and packed in barrels at the Cashmere plant in the summer of 1968. Once it got started, the new endeavor seemed to develop a life of its own and stayed around. A small tonnage of pears was also processed in the fall of 1969.

Meanwhile, the marketing and the R&D staffs were hard at work developing a viable product for distribution. The first success came in frozen concentrated cider, a mix of apple and pear concentrates, and next came the use of pears as a natural fruit sweetener in solid form for the

Washington's First Apple Family

Tom Auvil.

No other family has contributed more to the Washington apple industry than the Auvils. The present chair of the Tree Top Board of Directors is Thomas D. Auvil, who has served on that body since 1988, including a previous term as chair. As with other members of the extended clan, Tom Auvil has spent most of his adult life involved in some phase of the orchard business. With a BS degree in Horticulture from Washington State University, he is a research horticulturist with the Washington Tree Fruit Research Commission at Wenatchee and takes an active management role in a 50-acre family orchard at Orondo.

The family's story in Washington began when Tom Auvil's grandfather, Llewellyn Auvil, and his four brothers loaded all their possessions in a boxcar and left West Virginia, headed westward. Llewellyn settled down in Entiat, Washington, and, in 1928, he and his three sons, Grady, David, and Robert (Tom's father), borrowed most of the $11,000 purchase price for 150 acres of land at Orondo near Wenatchee. At first they planted 22 acres in apple trees and started what became the famous Auvil Fruit Company. The firm gradually expanded its orchard holdings until by 1940 it had about 40 acres of trees, and by the 1990s, more than 1,000 acres.

The oldest son, Grady Auvil, became renowned in the Washington fruit industry for his progressive production methods and his keen understanding of marketing. Acclaimed as a "Latter Day Johnny Appleseed," his accomplishments included the introduction of the Granny Smith variety of apples, the Rainier cherry, and the Fuji apple. After a friend declared that people who ate a new kind of peach he was growing would exclaim, "Gee Whiz, that is a good piece of fruit," the Auvil company started marketing its fruit under the "Gee Whiz" label. A recent documentary film on Grady Auvil and the family's contributions has that trademark title in capital letters, "GEE WHIZ." He was known not only for innovative ideas, but for his philanthropy, most notably an estate endowment of $2.9 million by him and his wife, Lillie, to fund scholarships and research at Washington State University and Wenatchee Valley College. In December 1998, Grady Auvil died at age 93, a few months after receiving the Washington Medal of Merit, the state's highest honor.

Tom Auvil's branch of the family sold its interest in the Auvil Fruit Company in 1973. Today, the firm is an employee-owned corporation. As a tribute to the organization that Grady Auvil and the Auvil family built, the company is still a leading innovator in the tree fruit industry.

---

industrial ingredients trade. Eventually, pear concentrate as a blend and natural sweetener for a variety of juices became a staple at Tree Top. It was this use that gave pears an important role in the cooperative's operations. Bill Charbonneau had laid down the rule that, unlike the despicable "belly-wash" beverages, sugar must not be added to Tree Top products. Reliance on pear concentrate as a natural sweetener instead of refined sugar was in keeping with Charbonneau's legacy.

In a broader context, Tree Top's development of a market for cull pears was an achievement almost comparable with what the cooperative had done for once-discarded apples. And this contribution, although involving smaller tonnages and less money, created an additional lucrative outlet and helped stabilize prices from top to bottom in the overall Washington fruit industry. Consequently, in 1972, Tree Top made contracts with pear growers that assured them of a ready market and fair prices ($15 per ton that year). At first these contracts were similar to those made with apple growers, but stipulated a cash basis only and did not include membership in the cooperative for those orchardists not already enrolled.

In time, besides the standard apple-pear combination, pear concentrate sweetener would lead the way for Tree

Top to market various other apple juice blends, including those using grapes, cherries, and cranberries as well as a separate pear-grape beverage.[6] An obvious advantage of these combinations was an increased volume of sales, and accordingly, additional profits returned to the grower-owners. A less noticeable benefit, in the processing stage, was determined by the price of the main components at a given time. That is, the ratio of the components in a blend could be adjusted up or down consistent with the "Brix scale," a scientific measurement involving the sweetening content at a certain temperature in the manufacturing process. One of the cooperative's first blends was 51 percent pear and 49 percent grape, but, because of the rising price of grapes purchased from outside sources, it later evolved into a 60-40 combination. Moreover, one of the main factors contributing to Tree Top's growth was the increasing cost of sugar, which influenced the price of competitors' sugared juices and soft drinks, making them more expensive. Another plus was an increasing public antipathy toward sugared beverages because of dietary concerns. Naturally sweetened drinks, such as those marketed by Tree Top, would become great favorites of health-minded consumers.

Tree Topics (January 1973).

It would take several years, however, for the realization of all these benefits. In the meantime, the future for processed pears remained a big question mark. This "problem," which would soon become a blessing, had occurred on B.C. Robbins's watch, although the project had been initiated earlier by James Klahre. In short, Robbins took "the rap" for the temporary dilemma of what to do with pear concentrate. Some critics even hinted that Robbins, by his tacit approval of pear concentrate as a natural sweetener, had disregarded Bill Charbonneau's decree against artificially sweetened beverages.

The board of directors seemed more concerned with conditions at the newly acquired Wenatchee plant than anything else. And they could get few satisfactory explanations from the general manager. Despite such difficulties in communication with the board, Robbins could count some notable accomplishments during his tenure. He updated the organizational chart introduced by Klahre, clearly delineating the reporting responsibilities of a growing number of management positions. Of special interest, a committee recommended against the production of apple sauce under the Tree Top label, and the full board agreed. Board president Wilbur Nelson had long called for better communication with the growers, and a newsletter entitled *Tree Topics* and edited by executive secretary Florence Martin, began publication on September 30, 1968. At first issued every other month, then monthly, it has remained an official organ of the cooperative and the most widely circulated compilation of news about its activities. Most important, Robbins's prize acquisition of the Wenatchee plant, although questioned at the time, had opened the way for significant expansion and diversification of Tree Top operations.

Yet problems often seemed to start at the Wenatchee plant. In August 1968, shortly before his departure from Tree Top, Robbins gave his approval for the managers (still the former owners) at the Wenatchee facility to buy 4,000 tons of apples on the open, cash market at no more than $40 a ton. The board had concurred with the decision. Significantly this was the first purchase of apples not under contract in Tree Top's short history as a grower-owned cooperative. This deviation also became associated with Robbins's watch, and somehow it was further connected to the unwelcome news arriving in the fall that processing apples would be in short supply. Drastic adjustments had to be made in production schedules and marketing programs, which particularly affected the relatively expensive plans for distribution of frozen concentrate. All advertising was stopped, and prices were sharply increased to maintain allocated shelf and freezer space in the stores. Again, Bill Charbonneau and his obsession with concentrate were vindicated when that product had the best sales rate, partly because it had no real competition from other brands.[7] The immediate tempest

Tree Topics (April 1973).

over the flow of raw product, one of many related to the "variables" in the supply pipeline, eventually blew over, and Tree Top emerged in relatively good condition.

Given the uncertainties at Tree Top in the post-Charbonneau period, Bud Robbins did not survive long as general manager. His tenure as general manager lasted only about 15 months. From all outward appearances, the board meeting on April 25, 1968, seemed to follow the usual agenda. Robbins and his department heads gave their reports, and other routine matters came up for discussion. At the close of the regular session, however, everyone else was excused and the board members stayed in their places. After a long discussion, a motion was approved by unanimous vote to ask for the resignation of Robbins. It was also decided that sales manager Ernie Stafford would become interim general manager, and that a search to fill the top position on a permanent basis would begin immediately.

In one crucial area Robbins had achieved notable success; he got along well with the executives of the Spokane Bank for Cooperatives. In fact, while he fell short of the Tree Top board's expectations, the bank was satisfied with him. Bank officials had heard rumors that Robbins was absorbed with affairs at the troubled Wenatchee plant, and that he wanted to make that facility much like his former place of employment with Welch Grape. With their financial involvement in Tree Top at stake, the Spokane bankers on occasion had advised him to take it easy. Toward the end, although he still had good relations with the bank, Robbins became essentially estranged from the Tree Top directors, and his lines of communication with them had broken down.

The Tree Top directors had experienced a time of frustration and rapid change in which they had often been forced to take day-by-day control of routine operations. The dramatic departure of Charbonneau, followed by the interim status of Klahre, then the brief tenure of Robbins, and afterwards another interim period with Stafford—all of these quick rotations caused disruptions. The time was approaching when the directors would have to back off from mundane decision-making and devote themselves instead to the determination of broad, long-term policies. In addition, most of them owned and operated large orchards that claimed their close attention. The frequent trips to Selah, often from considerable distances and at a sacrifice of their own affairs, had demonstrated their belief in the cooperative cause. But the directors simply did not have the time to hover over Tree Top and care for it on a regular basis. The cooperative was gaining maturity, but it was still short on stability and continuity. What the board and the grower-owners they represented needed was a general manager who could do the job of daily decision-making and free the directors to focus on policy-making. 🍎

Endnotes

1. Alfred Max Neubert, "A Study of the Effect of Filtration, Clarification, and Concentration on the Composition and Properties of Apple Juice," Ph.D. dissertation, State College of Washington, 1941, 4, 64–77; *Yakima Morning Herald*, March 20, 1963, 1.
2. Actually, this juice had been concentrated from Washington apples in a USDA laboratory at Chestnut Hills, Pennsylvania, and brought by the government officials to the Yakima annual meeting, where local water was added. *Yakima Morning Herald*, March 20, 1963, 15.
3. For a detailed description of apple cooperatives and their functions in the United States, see Gilbert W. Biggs, *Cooperatives in the Apple Industry*, Cooperative Marketing and Purchasing Division, Agricultural Cooperative Service, U.S. Department of Agriculture, Washington, D.C., September 1987.
4. For early apple growing in Oregon, see two articles by Joseph W. Ellison, "The Beginnings of the Apple Industry in Oregon," *Agricultural History* 11 (October 1937), 322–43, and "The Cooperative Movement in the Oregon Apple Industry, 1910–1929," *Agricultural History* 13 (April 1939), 77–96.
5. This quote and most of the information on pear concentrate came from *Tree Topics*, September 30, 1968, and June 1972.
6. Blends such as pear-apple and pear-grape are no longer produced by Tree Top, but many of the cooperative's juices still contain pear concentrate.
7. It was during these difficult times that the "two-pool system" for apple varieties was started at Wenatchee. In brief, this system placed a higher premium on, and paid more for, "peelers" used in industrial ingredients than for "juicers" used in juices.

With the New West Tree Top label prominently displayed, this promotional piece appeared in the *Los Angeles Times, Portland Oregonian, San Francisco Examiner*, and the *Seattle Post-Intelligencer*, November 9, 1947.

Magazine advertisement appearing in *Family Circle* and *Sunset*, November 1947, and *Western Family*, November 6, 1947.

Ads specifically targetting mothers.

In early 1957, a Safeway store display in San Francisco uses an image from a TV Bee Animated Spot to promote a 50 case display of 46 oz. Tree Top Apple Juice.

Helicopter display during the Halloween season.

The *Los Angeles Times, Portland Oregonian, San Francisco Examiner,* and the *Seattle Post-Intelligencer* ran this ad on January 11, 1948.

For people who know their apples.

This juice is as <u>pure</u> as the day
we picked the Jonathans, Winesaps
and Delicious apples in our

Washington State
orchards.

Tree Top's Pure Frozen Concentrated Apple Juice now carries the delicious taste of Washington's wonderful apples to 41 states and Canada. Packed in 6 and 12 oz. colorful lithographed cans.

The "Old Apple Tree"
Vancouver, Washington

A recent view of the Old Apple Tree, located near downtown Vancouver.

Jessica Antoine, Vancouer Urban Forestry

The first apple tree in the Pacific Northwest probably grew at Fort Vancouver—the Hudson's Bay Company's fur-trading post established in 1825, now the site of Vancouver, Washington. A reputed offspring of the original tree still bears fruit on the same spot. The historical significance of this tree, hailed locally as "the matriarch of Washington State's apple industry," recently forced highway designers to relocate their first choice for a major freeway interchange because it threatened to obliterate the site.

An early fanciful tale of the tree's origins has a decidedly romantic twist. It involves a dinner attended by several young HBC employees in London on the evening before their departure for the Oregon Country, then largely controlled by the British. According to this version:

One young lady at the party, smitten with the young gentleman beside her, saved the seeds from the apples served at dinner, gently wrapped them in paper, and tucked them into the man's vest pocket as a token of remembrance. Upon his arrival at Fort Vancouver, the young man discovered the seeds and gave them to the company's gardener for planting.

A similar but less sentimental account maintains that an HBC sea captain, Aemilious Simpson, planted seeds for the tree himself in 1827. Supposedly, he had saved the seeds in his vest pocket at a dinner party in London just before sailing for the Northwest Coast. Other stories claim it was 1826 and someone else planted the seeds—no one knows for sure.

Regardless, Narcissa Whitman, the wife of Dr. Marcus Whitman, noted the presence of apple trees at Fort Vancouver in 1836. Dr. Whitman took seeds from these trees and planted them east of the Cascades at their mission station, Waiilatpu, near present-day Walla Walla. By the mid 1840s, the Whitman's irrigated garden and orchard included 75 apple trees. Seeds were also planted at other early white settlements, including the Catholic mission at Ahtanum near Yakima, although reportedly these seeds came from France.

The Vancouver community has honored its "Old Apple Tree" in every way imaginable. In 1934, when President Franklin D. Roosevelt came to the Northwest for an inspection tour of the Grand Coulee Dam construction site, local officials contributed some of the tree's apples for a pie presented to the president upon his arrival in Portland. The site of the Old Apple Tree is now a public park. An annual Old Apple Tree Festival, typically held in early October, was discontinued for a few years, but was back on schedule in 2009. The festival focuses on historical and environmental themes with a number of activities for both kids and adults, including an apple-pie baking contest. Cuttings from the tree are given to visitors. In June 2009, the tree suffered serious damage when two of its main limbs snapped, but experts were called in for consultation, and the central section is still thriving.[1]

Donna Howard Jacky of Vancouver holding an apple pie she made from apples off the historic tree.

---

1. *Vancouver Columbian*, October 2, 27, 2009.

Grady Auvil.

John Auvil and the Auvil family.

Ross Packing Company calendar, 1939.

Tree Top Annual Report (October 1980).

Chapter 3

New Horizons

The guiding hand of the Spokane Bank for Cooperatives again came into play with the selection of Tree Top's next general manager. Robert E. Ward had been manager of the Gresham Berry Growers in Oregon when that firm merged with United Flav-R-Pac Growers of Salem, which already had established leadership in the market. He became assistant manager of the firm and ran its Gresham plant. The Spokane bank executives, who knew Ward and his record, suggested to him that he submit his resume to the Tree Top directors, who were encouraged to give it careful consideration. If the board decided to hire Ward, the bankers confided, he would be a "satisfactory" choice. It was good advice, resulting in the longest service yet of a Tree Top general manager, from August 1969 to October 1982.

Significantly, during Ward's tenure the cooperative gradually but perceptibly matured as its directors eased into a policy-making role and relinquished the routine duties of management. An advocate of vigorous executive leadership, Bob Ward believed that Tree Top must enter new endeavors to keep ahead of the competition. His plans included expanded marketing internationally, as well as domestically, and creating production alliances in other states. The 12-member board of directors, although united in moving toward a policy-making mode, sometimes had differences of opinion, as might be expected in a group of that size. For instance, there was a split in philosophy between those directors who were more willing to follow the lead of the manager and build the firm bigger and faster, as opposed to those more conservative members who wanted to proceed slower and keep expenses down. In short, the second group was less interested in becoming the "Minute Maid of Apple Juice" because of the financial risks involved. These differences surfaced periodically to hinder Ward's expansive "vision" for Tree Top's scope of operations. Nevertheless, under his forceful leadership, an impressive pattern of growth and profitability characterized this period, overshadowing internal differing viewpoints.

Robert E. Ward.
Tree Top Annual Report (October 1973).

In part to signify Ward's style of management, the board gave him the title of president as well as general manager in 1972. At this time, the titles of board leadership also were changed from president and vice president to chairman and vice chairman, and the annual meeting was shifted from March to November. In a notable action indicating Tree Top's expanding scope, the board also named E.M. "Whit" Whiteaker, formerly head of sales at the Portland Canning Company, as national sales manager of industrial products, with the responsibility of marketing evaporated and dehydrated products as well as apple and pear bulk concentrate. This unit was a forerunner of the industrial ingredients trade, today's sales leader. Actually, Ward's new designation as president also recognized Tree Top's standing as a major player in national food manufacturing. This made it easier for him to represent the firm in the industry as an equal, and thus more effectively, when dealing with other CEOs.

Previously, in the late 1960s, Tree Top had adopted a "chain of command" headed by the general manager and an assistant general manager, with designated divisions for such functions as sales, accounting, purchasing, personnel, grower relations, quality control, and plant managers. As the cooperative grew and its operations became more complex, the board had authorized this formation of a management team resembling the executive structure of the big private corporations. By 1980, when a thorough overhaul occurred, the leadership team included the president, a senior vice president, and six other vice presidents as well as departmental divisions for field services, sales, and plant managers. Now the board often referred to "management" as a group instead of singling out only the president.

Bob Ward's own concept of his new title soon appeared in tangible forms. He emphasized the necessity of planning for more than a year at a time, shifting to a long-range basis that would make Tree Top a "full service processor," taking all the raw product its growers could provide, as well as additional tonnages from other sources. The record showed, he reminded the grower-owners in December 1971, that the cooperative had "grown like topsy" in its first decade, which was only a slight exaggeration. Actually, Tree Top had experienced steady but comparatively modest growth in sales from $1.3 million in 1961 to $7.1 million in 1969–70; the spectacular advances would come in the 1970s.

Regardless, by the end of its first decade the cooperative was well on its way toward becoming the number one processor of fresh and concentrated apple juice in the United States, as well as a significant producer of evaporated and dehydrated fruit. Such progress, Ward said, had resulted from sound marketing, dedicated promotion, targeted advertising, and the introduction of the most modern equipment. New products had kept the firm ahead of the competition, but it must constantly stay on the lookout for additional opportunities to increase the list. "One thing for sure," Ward concluded, "there is no standing still; we will 'keep moving.'" A year later the enterprising executive proudly stated that Tree Top apple juice was on track to match the Welch brand in grapes. In fact, he declared, the cooperative was becoming so successful that it might soon have to turn away additional members wanting to share the attractive profits.

Ward's dedication to growth, and his emphasis on developing a full-service processor, signified the theme of Tree Top's second decade. During the 1970s and early 1980s, the company had its ups and downs and faced new challenges every year, but it still compiled an unprecedented record. In measured succession the cooperative acquired competing or complementary firms, remodeled and expanded manufacturing installations as well as warehouse facilities, and bolstered its product lineup and marketing areas. More than anything else, this fast-paced tempo of change indicated that the processing cooperative was becoming a "big fish" in the business world. But one question remained: could a regional cooperative in the far

Northwest corner of the country compete in the national marketplace for a sales prize totaling $2.5 billion against huge corporations with unlimited bankrolls for product promotion and advertising?

Previously, Tree Top had considered purchasing the Valley Evaporating Company, but, after a thorough investigation of the firm's operations, the board rejected the opportunity to buy this fruit-drying concern. Timing was important, and the acquisition of Valley Evap became more appropriate several years later. In 1976, however, as a logical part of its current growth strategy, the expanding cooperative bought the Ross Packing Company in Selah from New York-state based Seneca Foods Corporation for $2.3 million. The acquisition of this evaporated apple-drying plant, located near Tree Top's juice facility in Selah, gave the firm the capacity to handle larger tonnages of juice and peeler fruit from the Yakima Valley. As a complementary facility, the Ross plant in the south matched the Wenatchee unit's similar operations in that northern valley. Long recognized as a promising field, the evaporation of apples was now wide open for Tree Top's innovative research and development staff to explore for a wide range of new products.[1]

Unexpectedly, it became necessary to rebuild the structures and modernize the equipment at two existing plants when disastrous fires struck at Cashmere in August 1970, and Wenatchee in February 1976. In the case of Cashmere, which specialized in concentrates, the decision was made to continue operations under a temporary roof until the reconstruction was finished. This prevented the disposal of several thousand tons of apples at sacrificial prices. The destructive blaze at Wenatchee had started soon after another smaller fire was extinguished, with the bigger conflagration gutting the main building and its smoke causing costly damage to products stored in two nearby warehouses. By December 1976, a new $3-million facility with the most modern and efficient equipment available was in full operation at Wenatchee, which turned out a variety of dehydrated items.

Arson was suspected as the cause of both fires, especially at Wenatchee, although outside investigators found no proof in either case. A long, tedious lawsuit with the insurance carrier, mainly over the possibility of arson as well as Tree Top's responsibility for the Wenatchee conflagration, ended in favor of the cooperative and a settlement in excess of $2 million. However, it had taken countless hours for the headquarters staff to prepare the required court documents for the prolonged litigation.

Other expansion or new construction projects included a headquarters office building in Selah, which was completed in 1971, and a large addition to the Cashmere plant in 1980. Also, the original facility at Selah, where Bill Charbonneau began operations in 1944, was replaced by a new processing plant in 1973. Significantly, the rebuilt Cashmere site later added a 700,000-gallon tank farm for the bulk storage of concentrate at constant temperatures, a great advantage over individual drums at unregulated temperatures. Bulk storage also helped regulate the flow of raw product for processing, but, of course, could not eliminate altogether the uncertainties of the supply pipeline from the growers.

Back when Bill Charbonneau started his private company, he had sold only apple juice in six sizes. By the early 1980s, Tree Top could boast a steadily increasing multitude of products with various flavors for retail consumers and industrial food concerns alike. As Bob Ward described Tree Top's progress and potential in the 1970s, "It's like a big black bear running down a hill. A bear only has a small tail, but we're gonna have to grab ahold of that thing and really hang on. When it gets moving, we can't let go. That's how big this is." It was an imaginative analogy, and largely accurate.

In fact, the bounds of expansion at times seemed unlimited. In the early 1970s, the Tree Top management and board considered the formation of "a multi-product marketing organization" that would process most, or at least a large part, of all the fruit and vegetables grown in the Pacific Northwest. It all might start with the canning of pears. Support for this ambitious umbrella-like goal, however, apparently disappeared soon after former general manager James E. Klahre submitted a study in 1973, pointing out the limitations of the market for canned Bartlett pears. In this decade, as already indicated, Tree Top did emphasize the development of pear concentrates and blends, marketing pear-apple, pear-grape, and pear-apple cider drinks. In another pioneering break-

through with pears, besides the earlier innovative processing of whole pear culls, Tree Top began buying "soft pears," or the slurry waste from canneries. Prior to this time the slurry, much like the earlier disposal of cull apples, had been hauled away and buried, or sold at giveaway prices for cattle feed.

To make profitable use of soft pears, when others had tried and failed, Tree Top researchers devised an involved $2.5-million process of changing the original raw product into puree, treating it with enzymes, and eventually achieving a concentrated form. The sale of installation rights to the manufacturing process itself, and also of soft pear concentrate, to other processors and competing firms, such as Del Monte and Snokist, became a profitable new market. An increased supply of pear concentrate to use in blends and an economical source of fruit sweetener stood out as advantages of this new field. Discerning consumers could easily determine the difference between pears for sweeteners as compared to sugar or other artificial substances.[2] Frozen pear and apple concentrates became highly profitable through sales on both the retail and industrial food markets. While the Cashmere plant specialized in frozen concentrates, the original Selah location produced blends, mainly regular or single strength juice, which was the cornerstone of retail sales.

Among the other marketing entries tried about this time were an apple-orange combination, frozen concentrated cider (an apple-pear combination), sparkling cider and "Sparkling Royale" (a pear-grape blend), sliced apple

Unloading apple bins at Selah.
Tree Top Annual Report (October 1980).

Tree Top Employees and Innovative Equipment

Tree Top employees familiar with the production process have often suggested changes or completely new designs for machinery. An example of these initiatives was the design devised by plant manager Kenneth A. Banks and plant supervisor Thomas P. Stokes for new peeling equipment after the destructive fire at Wenatchee in 1976. Before the conflagration, the plant had depended on leased peeling equipment with many moving parts, which was cumbersome and prone to breakdowns, frequently resulting in lost time for the entire facility. Basically, the old machinery consisted of a chain-and-bucket conveyor that carried apples through a caustic solution before dumping them where steam and water jets removed the skin. Fruit was sometimes bruised in this dumping stage.

Banks and Stokes had worked together at Lamb-Weston in Hermiston, Oregon, where peeling potatoes was a major operation. With the fire at Wenatchee giving them an opportunity to replace the old, leased equipment, they drew on their background experience with potatoes for an example of what might work on apples. It was hardly an easy task because apples tend to float on the surface in liquid, while potatoes sink, not to mention that apples bruise more easily and are more sensitive to heat and chemicals. After a month of planning, Banks and Stokes settled on a design featuring a rotating reel that moved the fruit through a circulating caustic solution before gently floating it into the peeling process. A machine shop spent another month turning Banks and Stokes's design into operational equipment. Once in place, the new machinery handled three or four times more fruit than the previous system, took up one-fourth of the floor space, and ran on only two electric motors instead of the 16 previously required. "On top of all that," reported the cooperative's publication *Tree Topics*, "Wenatchee is experiencing a considerable decrease in mechanical down-time, operational costs, [and] manpower utilized in cleanup."[1]

The new equipment drew widespread attention. It was patented by Tree Top and a California company was licensed as the manufacturer. The Selah-based firm was soon receiving royalties on sales from as far away as Italy. Tom Stokes had been at Tree Top only about a year when he started working on this important project in 1976. He has been president and CEO of the cooperative since 1999.

---

1. *Tree Topics*, October 1977.

pie filling, frozen fruit juice bars, fresh-apple products, apple sauce, and cherry and grape concentrate. With the widespread demand for organic and health foods, Tree Top responded by developing a product designated as "natural" or "unfiltered" apple juice, which bypassed the usual filtering process. Introduced in 1971, this new item had outstanding success in Southern California where the popularity of natural and weight-control products ran especially high. Tree Top's longstanding claims of "Pure" and "No Sugar Added" also had a special appeal for those consumers on diabetic diets and with other health concerns.

The ingredients market and similar outlets also flourished during this period with military contracts for apple sauce, the sale of dehydrated and low-moisture products to the giant conglomerates General Foods and Pillsbury, and purchases by other firms in the industrial foods industry. For example, the Wenatchee drying plant, with the slogan of "Slice 'em, dice 'em, chop 'em, or grate 'em," took cull apples, washed, peeled, and cored them, and then turned out sliced and diced items as well as flakes, granules, and powder. The ingredient products usually went to the industrial trade where they were used in cake mixes, fruit-flavored cereals, soft centers of hard candy, pie and pastry fillings, specialty doughnuts, "trail mixes," and the increasingly popular frozen TV dinners. The Ross drying facility at Selah also took peeler apples and, after coring and slicing, processed them into slices or bits for ingredient outlets. With the Ross and Wenatchee sites specializing in dried apple items, Tree Top could boast of becoming the largest supplier of this fruit product in the United States, and probably in the world. All four of the cooperative's facilities, with their specializations, gave Tree Top impressive market diversification.

Oregon orchardists had first held membership in the cooperative, with Idaho approved for the same status in July 1971. Tree Top had made an agreement with Diamond Fruit Growers of Hood River, Oregon, to process some of its pears for concentrate. The Selah-based firm had also reached out beyond the Pacific Northwest to make similar joint packing arrangements in more distant states. In an abortive attempt to establish production in the South, Tree Top provided technical assistance to Fenwick Apple Products, which constructed a processing facility at Gay, Georgia. This initiative resulted in a joint marketing agreement that authorized use of the Tree Top label. The Georgia firm's owner, however, suddenly died of a heart attack at his home while a Tree Top representative was there conferring with him. As a further complication, the Fenwick company had financial problems that could reflect unfavorably on Tree Top.

In addition, the Fenwick concern had obtained apples from North Carolina, a state that followed U.S. Department of Agriculture grading standards for that fruit, while Washington state had different, even higher standards. At about this time, Tree Top planned to make a co-packing agreement with a prospective processing plant in North Carolina. These plans and entanglements with Fenwick in Georgia surfaced indirectly in a classic textbook interpretation by the Supreme Court of the U.S. Constitution's commerce clause. A North Carolina statue, in effect, prohibited the visual display of Washington grades on fruit entering the state. In the much-cited *Hunt* case (1977), the Court held that the law was an unconstitutional restriction of commerce, and not in the national interest "insofar as it affected the interstate shipment of Washington apples."[3] Despite this victory, North Carolina's prejudicial view of Washington apples influenced the Tree Top board of directors to reject the planned co-packing arrangement in that state by a narrow vote.

Contractual agreements in other states to bottle, re-pack, and co-pack would work out more smoothly, such as those with Citrus World in Lake Wales, Florida; the privately owned Cherry Hills Orchards and the Cherry Growers cooperative, both in Michigan; and the Albion Cooperative of New York state. When marketed, these products carried the Tree Top label and met its strict specifications for quality and taste. Tree Top made similar deals inside the Pacific Northwest region and across the Canadian border with British Columbia Tree Fruits, Ltd., otherwise known as Sun-Rype Products. The reasons for these connections arose from various motivations. First, there was the geographical imperative of obtaining better shipping rates at locations closer than the Pacific Northwest to distant population centers. Then came the current compelling objective to make Tree Top a "national brand." Also, in keeping with its central mission, there was the obligation to open as many marketing opportunities as possible for the grower-owners.

Because of its role as a cooperative, the Selah-based firm apparently considered, but rejected, an obvious solution to its geographical location and the difficulties of going nationwide. Tree Top could have formed an integrated joint distribution system with a large private corporation, such as Ocean Spray, Coca-Cola, or Pillsbury. But the danger of being swallowed up in a subsidiary status instead of becoming a real partner probably outweighed the advantages.[4] In the early 1970s, Tree Top did begin exploring the opportunities offered by foreign export markets, but pursuing this kind of expansion depended largely on the availability of raw product for processing.

An enterprising research and development program, combined with vigilant quality control, stood behind the impressive expansion of product lines. Periodically R&D submitted a list of research projects for prospective new, marketable items. For instance, in 1978 the research staff listed as high priorities for consideration a sparkling apple juice or blend, which soon became a reality, and a cherry-cranberry blend and a pure cranberry drink, both of which were tested but not marketed; nor was a potential "raisin-like apple product" mixed with nuts to be called "Cravens" sent to the grocery store shelves. R&D also played a major role in the production of the soft pear concentrate and unfiltered apple juice that achieved huge popularity in the dominant Los Angeles marketing area.

Strict standards of quality control had been ingrained in the Tree Top culture by Bill Charbonneau. The firm increased its efforts to maintain those standards through the technical services manager and trained personnel stationed in laboratories at the various plants. In short, it was their duty to guarantee that Charbonneau's legacy, embodied in the current slogan "Tastes Like a Fresh Apple," rang true throughout the entire production process. Because of current public interest in every aspect of food processing, quality control spent considerable time answering consumer inquiries about products and requests for nutritional information.

Tree Top also relied on the nearby state land-grant universities for research services and consulting work by their scientists. As previously pointed out, Dr. Alfred M. Neubert, who had done pioneering research involving concentrated apple juice at the State College of Washington in Pullman (now Washington State University), advised Bill Charbonneau in his successful quest for concentrate. Later, while Robert M. Dennis served as vice president of field services, he collaborated in various studies with the

U.S. Department of Agriculture and served on the International Apple Institute's board of directors. Dennis also developed a close working relationship with Dr. Desmond O'Rourke of the IMPACT Center at WSU in formulating predictions of upcoming apple crops. Likewise, agricultural scientists at Oregon State University in Corvallis provided helpful information and advice. Other outside professional consultants were often hired to study industrial, labor relations, or management problems and submit reports of their recommendations.

Energetic marketing and sales initiatives by the cooperative's own staff, assisted by experienced professional advertising and promotional agencies, spearheaded the expansion into new marketing areas and the introduction of new product lines. The Tree Top brand name became a household word synonymous with apple juice itself, and the cooperative sold more under that familiar label than all the other one-label processors combined in the 11 western states. By the mid-1970s, well-planned promotional efforts had helped make Tree Top apple juice, with its hallmark bright green label and two big red apples, the market leader in the Midwest, Southwest, and Southeast—41 states in all, including Alaska and Hawaii, in addition to some outlets in western Canada. Only the 9 northeastern states remained for future campaigns, one of which was not long in coming.

From the time the trees first showed buds, field representatives out in the various orchard areas of the Northern and Southern divisions kept in continual communication with the growers and warehouse owners to make predictions about how much fruit would be available. Most growers contracted their processing fruit through warehouses, while others chose to haul it themselves, sometimes a bin at a time, to a Tree Top facility. At the Selah juice plant alone crews could load 15 semi-trucks and 8 railroad cars simultaneously, and it took 110 trucks a day to bring in the raw product and supplies for operations there. Forty-five strategically located brokers managed the distribution of the cooperative's products. Fluctuating transportation costs, especially for tanker trucks during the oil crisis of the late 1970s, always demanded close attention. Not surprisingly, because of the difference in freight rates, sales of regular, or single strength, apple juice was limited to the western states and Canada, while the compact concentrated juice held sway in distant markets beyond Denver.

Advertising was nothing new for Tree Top; Bill Charbonneau had hired a national sales manger and launched expensive television campaigns. Now the company moved to the next level, beginning with 30-second network television commercials on the *Today Show* and Johnny Carson's *Tonight Show*, as well as shorter spots on daytime television and during prime-time evening movies. Additional exposure came in women's magazines and newspapers and on the menus of some 1,000 Denny's restaurants nationwide that listed "Tree Top Apple Juice" among the four juice choices. Denny's was considered a "major breakthrough" because it tapped the lucrative "eating-out trade." Likewise, Tree Top targeted the fast food services in convenience stores, of which 35,000 to 40,000 were springing up across the country. And a regional airline's "Seat Occupied" cards offered Tree Top as one of the juices available to passengers.

None of these promotional forays, however, matched the enthusiasm that accompanied the opening of the New York City marketing area in early 1981. The cooperative's insiders dubbed it "Tree Top's March to the East," or alternatively, "The Big Apple Goes to the Big City." The 1981 annual report featured a full-page illustration with a giant container of Tree Top apple juice astride Manhattan, proclaiming at the top, "The Big Apple Is Here," and below, "America's #1 Selling Apple Juice, Tree Top." Significantly, as the cooperative's publication *Tree Topics* pointed out: "For the first time Tree Top will not bear the burden of building apple juice consumption in a newly-opened area [e.g., earlier in Southern California] as New York City is the largest apple juice market in the nation. Each resident of New York City averages consuming over one case of apple juice per person per year."[5]

Until this time, prohibitive shipping rates had made it impossible to enter the East Coast market, but now products could be transported economically from the "satellite operation in Michigan."[6] Management believed that this prospective marketing triumph was, according to *Tree Topics*, "the last giant step toward making Tree Top a national brand." One slight problem spoiled the celebration—the old story of an unpredictable supply pipeline. The raw product available simply fell far short of the volume required to manufacture goods for such an expanded market. Consequently, under the added impact of a severe national recession, the triumphant march turned into retreat, which resulted in a geographically restricted

Tree Top's Invasion of New York City

FIRST SERIES NATIONAL TELEVISION ADVERTISING

Tree Top goes national.

- First National Advertising on all three networks.

abc CBS NBC

- Generating over 1.2 Billion Gross Impressions.
- Creating national demand for Tree Top 100% Pure Fruit Juice Products.
- Seen on these National Game Shows . . .

the Price is Right	FAMILY FEUD Day and Night	CARD SHARKS
The Newlywed Game	WHEEL of FORTUNE	HIGH ROLLERS
password + plus	THE $20,000 PYRAMID	THE HOLLYWOOD SQUARES

Tree Top Annual Report (November 5, 1980).

THE BIG APPLE IS HERE.

AMERICA'S #1 SELLING APPLE JUICE. TREE TOP.

Tree Top Annual Report (November 4, 1981).

In the late 1970s, Tree Top laid plans to establish a full-fledged nationwide marketing system. The cooperative's apple juice had become the best selling brand in 41 states, with only the 9 northeastern states remaining to be conquered. The next step in this ambitious strategy of expansion called for a concerted promotional assault on the prime target in the unconquered territory—New York City. To establish a footing in the "Big Apple," however, the Selah-based cooperative had to force its way into that huge eastern urban market where several big corporate giants already were engaged in a turf war among themselves. President Robert E. Ward explained the situation in the 1981 annual report:

We have and are completing opening all U.S. markets. This has been costly. Eastern processors do not want us back there and fight us. These markets are a necessity as there is no other home for the Washington processed apple. There are too many pro-

cessed apples in the West to be marketed there…This means we must continue to build our own outlets for Washington State juice.

It was the boldest expansion Tree Top had attempted so far.

In anticipation of the New York venture, the cooperative mounted an impressive and expensive nationwide advertising campaign. The prestigious McCann-Erickson agency, with headquarters in New York City, created a series of television commercials based on research into why consumers bought Tree Top products. All of the ads, which included spots on 10 popular game shows, concluded with the folksy punch line, "Tree Top—it always tastes like somebody cared." For the New York invasion itself, Tree Top increased the promotional tempo, using its own sales force as well as hired brokers and public relations venues.

After an all-out effort, however, Tree Top had to withdraw. Undoubtedly, the opposition of the big conglomerates already on the scene had some influence in the abortive endeavor. Also, the unfavorable economic conditions of the day, which caused a "flattening" of retail grocery sales, had an effect. But the main reason was that the supply pipeline of raw product failed to meet production goals for such an expanded market.

marketing outreach. The disappointed promoters soberly admitted, "We got our heads handed to us on a platter!"

Despite such setbacks, the record for the 1970s into the early 1980s had shown remarkable increases of production and profitability. When Bill Charbonneau promoted the formation of the cooperative in 1960, he had specified that the grower-members must pledge to deliver at least 30,000 tons of raw product for processing annually, but he had to settle for closer to 20,000 tons. In its first decade, while Tree Top fought to establish a niche in the apple juice market, the Selah-based firm routinely processed between 20,000 and 40,000 tons of fruit annually, and sales rose steadily from $1.3 million in 1961 to $7.1 million in 1969–70.

By the 1970s, a decade of spectacular growth when it captured 20 percent of national sales, Tree Top was handling tonnages of 140,000 to 160,000 a year, and, in fact, processed an unprecedented tonnage of about 252,000 in 1979. Sales also ballooned by an average of 20 percent a year, reaching $137 million in 1982, for an 11-fold increase in a decade. The record crops of the late 1970s had encouraged the management to march confidently into the New York City market. Another expression of confidence in the continued flow of the raw product pipeline came in March 1979 when Tree Top gave wide publicity to its "Million Pounder Program." Eight railroad cars were sent from Selah to Dallas loaded with 29,646 cases of apple juice weighing over a million pounds.

In 1978 the cooperative had not only handled its share of the largest apple crop so far in Washington history, but also accepted all that the fruit members could deliver and paid them all-time high returns. Skeptical growers had derided Charbonneau's prediction that they would someday get $100 a ton for their processing apples, but they received as much as $186 for the 1978–79 crop, and a year later, up to $200 per ton. As general manager, Charbonneau had angered the orchardists by shutting down the only plant then in Selah and refusing to receive any more fruit. Now, at least one of Tree Top's four facilities operated year-round.[7]

Two basic influences had helped stimulate these impressive developments. Consumer taste had shifted to healthy diets and natural fruit beverages, which played to Tree Top's specialized advantage. Also, the Selah-based firm had made a significant investment in frozen concentrate production,

which helped minimize transportation costs for national marketing. Unprecedented peacetime inflation of the late 1970s boosted retail prices of juice to new highs. But apparently because of brand loyalty and an appreciation of Tree Top's reputation for natural nutritional content, faithful grocery store customers seemed willing to pay more and the market base remained solid.

Tree Top's dramatic statistical increases had the downside of attracting giant conglomerates into the field. For instance, the food industry behemoth Pillsbury entered the market by purchasing a Minneapolis firm with an apple juice facility at Yakima.[8] Pillsbury's multi-million-dollar advertising budget gave a distinct advantage to its subsidiary, which soon began producing for national distribution. In fact, Pillsbury's new venture was an essential part of an interesting series of events. Besides an increasing national demand for apple juice (sometimes up 30 percent a year), the entry of Pillsbury resulted in heated competition for the limited supply of raw product, which, in turn, helped bring a $200-a-ton returns to growers. This price level, according to one informed source, was about $40 more a ton than expected locally, and $100 to $140 per ton more than processors in other regions were paying. The differences in the cost of raw product brought tough competition for Tree Top in retail venues outside the Pacific Northwest where raw product was cheaper.

The high prices for raw product, although a dream come true for growers, could become a problem, especially for the privately owned processors, who somehow had to turn a profit despite the backbreaking initial costs. In this situation Tree Top enjoyed some advantage because the grower-owners were both its suppliers, who reaped the high market prices, and its stockholders (or "stakeholders"), who received a share of whatever profits the market would return. This general situation, mainly the entry of Pillsbury into the field as a powerful competitor, had undoubtedly influenced Tree Top's attempt to meet this challenge by marching into New York City and going nationwide. The venture failed, but Tree Top still remained the biggest seller of apple juice in the country with 20 percent of the market.

By late 1981, the "chickens came home to roost," that is, the results of rapid growth and other factors caught up with Tree Top. As one cooperative executive put it: "The large crop years of 1979 and 1980 forced Tree Top to grow faster than it was financially capable of doing."[9] To accomplish

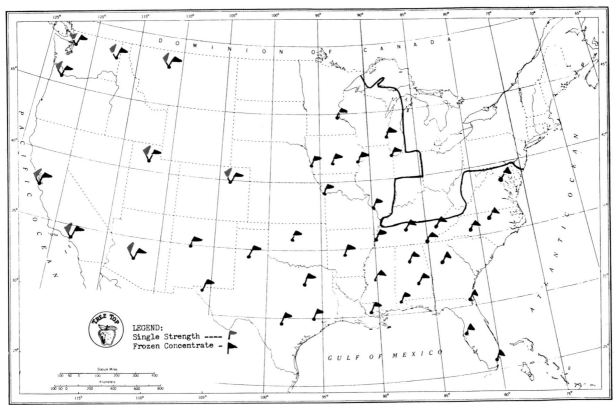

In 1973, Tree Top marketed single strength and/or frozen concentrated apple juices in 41 states, including Alaska and Hawaii. The flags represent 45 brokers—10 in the 11 western states and Alaska, 33 in the eastern and southern areas, and 1 each for the military and western Canada. During this period, Tree Top's sales department constantly received requests about apple juice availability for the northeastern states. Tree Top planned to enter this latter market when assured of an adequate supply of processing apples.

Tree Top Annual Report (October 1973).

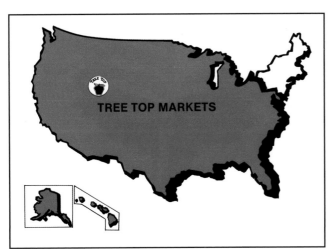

By 1980, the marketing of single strength and frozen concentrated juices had advanced further into the Northeast.

Tree Top Annual Report (October 1980).

Tree Top Annual Report (October 1973).

Tree Top Annual Report (October 1973).

Receiving and washing apples prior to crushing.
Tree Top Annual Report (October 1973).

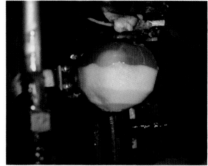

"Slice 'em, dice 'em, chop 'em, or grate 'em"—
In 1980, Tree Top's two apple drying plants in
Wenatchee and Selah were the largest suppliers of
dried apples in the nation, and possibly the world.
Tree Top Annual Report (October 1980).

Selah Juice Plant.
Tree Top Annual Report (October 1980).

Cashmere plant.
Tree Top Annual Report (October 1980).

One of our 30 million quality control experts.

It always tastes like somebody cared.

"Why Tree Top Is Number One," Tree Top Annual Meeting (November 4, 1981).

Henderson Luelling
Harbinger of Commercial Apple
Growing and Processing

Milwaukee, Oregon, mural.
Larry Kangas, mural artist; Robert West, photographer

The real harbinger of today's commercial fresh-apple trade, as well as the processing of that fruit in the Pacific Northwest, began in the Willamette Valley of western Oregon in 1847. Henderson Luelling, an experienced horticulturist, led an extraordinary family caravan from Iowa over the Oregon Trail that year.[1] He was accompanied by his pregnant wife, Elizabeth, and their eight children. Of his four wagons, the leading and largest one, fondly christened the "traveling nursery" and the "botanical ark," was so heavy it had to be pulled by three yoke of oxen. This unusual vehicle carried two big box-like containers, filled with charcoal and fertile Iowa soil because Luelling had discovered that this mixture held water reasonably well. In the oversized boxes, he had actually planted, not simply wrapped with cloth, 700 grafted trees, vines, and bushes, including 21 varieties of apple saplings.

The Luelling party traveled slowly, usually alone or with small wagon trains, to protect the valuable cargo from the rigors of the overland trail. Also, it took extra time to water the young trees every day by hand during dry spells without rain. A family member recalled that during the journey an Indian leader revealed that the traveling nursery supposedly had saved the party from attack because the "Great Spirit" in the trees had obviously placed the Leullings under special safekeeping. After seven months spent crossing broad prairies, rough mountain passes, and treacherous rivers, the Luellings arrived in Oregon with 400 or 500 surviving grafts, plus some seeds. Henderson Luelling soon found good land south of Portland near present-day Milwaukie, and started an orchard business. An Iowa neighbor, William Meek, later became a partner, as did a brother, Seth Luelling. According to a scholarly authority, this firm "established the first nursery of grafted fruit stock on the Pacific Coast." Henderson Luelling has been compared to Luther Burbank as one of "'the two great horticulturists of the west coast.'"[2]

The Luelling nursery developed a booming trade selling grafted apple trees to other settlers, who eagerly bought them for a dollar apiece, a substantial price on that frontier of bartering, where real money was scarce. The California gold rush, beginning in 1849, opened a lucrative market for Oregon's fresh apples as well as its trees. In 1865, Ezra Meeker obtained 1,500 young fruit trees at Milwaukie and took them north across the Columbia River to his home at Puyallup, Washington Territory. In the 1850s and 1860s,

frenzied mining activity in the "Inland Empire" east of the Cascades influenced the rise of small-scale commercial fruit cultivation in the Walla Walla area, the Okanogan country, and elsewhere near the camps. By about 1886, the first apple trees, probably descendants of Henderson Luellings' early grafts, had been planted in the Wenatchee Valley. The now-famous apple orchards of the Yakima and Wenatchee valleys started appearing in the late 19th and early 20th centuries.[3]

1. Of Welsh stock, Henderson's earlier family members had changed their name from Llewellyn to Lewelling upon arriving in the United States. He preferred it spelled as Luelling. His well-known brother, Seth—who at first used this last spelling in Oregon, but later changed back to Lewelling—is credited with developing the Bing cherry.

2. Thomas C. McClintock, "Henderson Luelling, Seth Lewelling, and the Birth of the Pacific Coast Fruit Industry," *Oregon Historical Quarterly* 68 (June 1967), 153–74. See also, Van Lanen, "'We Have Grown Fine Fruit," 30–36. For Luelling's contribution to economic development in Oregon, see John D. Unruh Jr., *Plains Across: The Overland Emigrants and the Trans-Mississippi West, 1840–60* (Urbana: University of Illinois Press, 1979), 390–91.

3. Otis W. Freeman, "Apple Industry of the Wenatchee Area," *Economic Geography* 10 (April 1934), 160–71.

its remarkable success in the marketplace, the cooperative had borrowed extensively for the expansion of production facilities. National economic conditions, most notably high inflation and a raging recession, had hit the Selah-based firm hard. For the 1979 and 1980 bumper harvests, the board approved management's decision to take the record tonnages, pay the growers unprecedented prices, process the raw material, store it, and try to find markets for the finished goods. To carry the extraordinarily large inventories, it became necessary to borrow large amounts of money at steep interest rates. Also, there was the financial stress caused by the advertising and promotional expenses of the unsuccessful march on New York City.

Even more unfortunate, returns to the growers suffered a sharp decline, from the previous bonanza tonnage prices of $186 and $200, down to a $50 range for the 1981 harvest. For the first time in 10 years, the cooperative had paid the growers less than the cash market average, and some dropped their membership. All of these accumulated circumstances resulted in a major transition, or reorientation, of operational policies to avoid a financial decline. After 20 years of focusing on production, the cooperative shifted its primary concern to the other end of the system, the demands of the marketplace. Above all, the perils of serving as a full-service processor, mainly the creation of large carryover inventories, had to be avoided by all means.

As usual, much of this change in direction had its roots in the old challenge of an unpredictable raw material supply. President Robert E. Ward lamented, "We never know ahead of time what kind of volume we'll have." In the early years, Tree Top might shut down its manufacturing facilities and go two or three months without any products available to send retailers. "You just don't do that in the food business," an experienced outside observer commented, "but somehow they did." When the cooperative had sold all it could produce from the supply pipeline of raw product, management usually shifted the emphasis to cutting costs and improving efficiency, but those measures had only a limited effect. Another remedy attempted for the supply problem involved a pilot project, in which a few members signed contracts promising to grow apples exclusively for processing, and none for the fresh-fruit trade. It did not to work because high fixed costs, such as for labor and irrigation water, required growers to produce primarily for the traditional fresh market and its more reliable

returns. As already mentioned, Tree Top also moved ahead with the processing of pears to increase the flow of raw product. None of these solutions brought lasting results.

President Bob Ward hit upon the remedy of buying large amounts of foreign apple concentrate on the world market to solve the ups and downs of the supply pipeline. He reasoned that concentrate could be purchased only when needed, and would stabilize production and bolster market commitments. [10] An important concern connected with the flow of raw product was the preservation of shelf space in retail grocery stores, which had to be purchased in a fierce rivalry with competing firms. This privilege was difficult to keep if a shortage of products occurred. With all these issues in mind, Ward bought large tonnages of foreign concentrate. Some drums arrived already damaged after transport by ship. Others deteriorated while in storage, sometimes leaking or blowing up, or because the bungs popped out. Barrels on occasion expanded, split their seams, and the contents ran onto the ground when trucks delivered them. And the loading docks sometimes had a coat of concentrate standing on them.

It was the old story of "feast or famine." With abundant stores of concentrate already on hand, the growers had flooded the supply pipeline with record-breaking tonnages of raw product. In the long run, then, the rapid growth of the 1970s, combined with a complex pattern of other forces, affected major purchasing and marketing decisions for years to come. Even before the impending financial crisis, the Spokane Bank for Cooperatives had demanded an overhaul of Tree Top's capitalization structure. After lengthy deliberation, the Selah-based concern's board of directors adopted what was called the Base Capital Fund to replace the previous Revolving Fund. In effect, the new plan, which had become effective in July 1977, provided a more dependable flow of operational funding by making each member's "Equity Share," or mandatory annual investment in the firm, dependent on a formula involving the individual's tonnage delivered over a six-year period. The new capitalization system had hardly taken hold, however, when the 1979–80 bumper crops and their financial repercussions struck.

In response, the board shored up the membership contract with a conditional pledge that the cooperative would be a full-service processor, as CEO Bob Ward had recommended, and accept all the fruit the growers could deliver. On the other hand, as the directors emphasized, the

Piled up St. Helens ash in Selah.

Eruption of Mount St. Helens
May 18, 1980

Mount St. Helens is the most active volcano among all the ominous cone-shaped peaks in the Cascade Range. Its last significant eruption had occurred 125 years before. Then, on May 18, 1980, the mountain blew off nearly 1,500 feet of its summit and released 1.4 billion cubic yards of ash that covered 22,000 square miles. The massive plume rose about 80,000 feet in 15 minutes, and in the next three days spread east across the nation. After passing over Washington, D.C., and the East coast, the sinister column moved on across the Atlantic Ocean. In 15 days it had circled the globe.

On that Sunday afternoon, a sunny spring day was suddenly turned into the dark of night in the region east of the Cascades. Heavy deposits of the grayish ash covered the ground for 300 miles downwind of the eruption. People feared leaving their homes and breathing the outside air. Many wore face masks reminiscent of the Great Flu Pandemic of 1918–19, and even health authorities were not certain about the permanent effects of the mysterious dust. Orchardists, fearing that their trees would be killed or damaged, sprayed water to clean the ash-laden limbs. National news accounts reported that the Yakima Valley, "in the path of the fall-out[,] was doomed and buried under a blanket of ash."[1]

As scientific reports minimized the harmful effects of the grayish material still on the ground, concerns about health problems subsided. In Selah, the debris was scooped up into several huge piles, including one near Main Street. Estimates varied on how much ash had fallen there and in other vicinities. In this instance, Tree Top could generalize that the Selah headquarters area had been deluged with 250 tons. For two more specific areas, the figures were more exact. Two sizable truck scales registered precisely 1,590 pounds of ash landing on their decks.

1. Robert S. Lince, *The Selah Story: History of Selah, East Selah, and Wenas Valley in Yakima County, Washington* (Selah: Selah Valley Optimist Printing, 1984), 197. See also, *Tree Topics*, June 1980.

members must do their part by bringing their eligible fruit to Tree Top every year, and not shop around in some years for a better price elsewhere.[11] The issue of member loyalty to the cooperative, addressed here head-on, remained a sensitive topic for years. Such were the "feast or famine" complexities of the supply pipeline.

Besides his large purchases of foreign concentrate and the various financial problems taking their toll, CEO Bob Ward had other difficulties as well.[12] Displeased with the abrupt decline in their returns after 1979–80, many grower-members loudly complained that the purchases of concentrate posed a threat to the market for their own crops. Equally important, Ward had fallen into disfavor with the Spokane Bank for Cooperatives because of the array of costly financial ventures. Showing the extent of their displeasure, the Spokane bankers threatened to cut off Tree Top's line of credit unless Ward was dismissed. Not surprisingly, then, Raymond E. Colbert, chair of the board of directors, announced in the 1982 annual report that President Robert E. Ward had "taken early retirement," and that Dennis J. Colleran, vice president of finance, had been appointed interim general manager.

Ray Colbert.

In June 1979, a local newspaper had stated, "The biggest development in the [Washington] apple industry today comes in processed apples," and went on to say that processing not only increased the income of orchardists, but helped stabilize prices in the fresh-fruit market as well. The article continued, "Much the largest in expanding the market for processing apples is Tree Top Inc.," with Robert Ward as president.[13] The implied connection between the importance of processing and the role of Tree Top's CEO gave Ward the recognition he deserved for his leadership and vision.

The end of the "Ward Era" (1969–82) seemed to inspire a series of reflective commentaries on Tree Top's accomplishments, problems, and future challenges. Most of these eulogies agreed that the cooperative's impressive growth in the 1970s had given the Washington apple industry the solid foundation that the overall structure had needed for so long. In December 1978, outgoing board chair

Raymond C. O'Neal of Chelan stated it emphatically: "We've put a floor under the fresh apple market where none had previously existed. Tree Top has [also] successfully developed the processing pear, just as it did the processing apple." When Orville Ormiston of Yakima retired in 1981, after 21 years as a board member, he sounded the same theme: "Tree Top is the most important thing in the Washington apple industry today." As proof, he said, the Spokane Bank for Cooperatives had given special attention to Tree Top because the bankers realized the crucial contributions of the Selah-based firm. With the large, new orchards in the Columbia Basin country, Ormiston observed, the apple business was in a transitory stage, and only time would tell what challenges lay ahead.

Reminiscing years later, long-time board member Raymond E. Colbert of Tonasket gave a great deal of credit for Tree Top's success to Bob Ward, who "had done wonders" as president with his rare talent of turning "an idea into reality." Without Ward, said Colbert, the cooperative would "never have gotten off the ground." As for the big picture, he asserted, Tree Top had not only undergirded the Washington apple industry, but had also bolstered the economy of the entire Pacific Northwest region. Using his own experience as an example, Colbert recalled that before Tree Top the highest price he ever received for cull apples was $15 a ton, and some years he had to pay out $5 a ton to get them hauled away. When growers started getting from $20 to $175 a ton, he chuckled, many of them simply said, "Well, that's what they're worth!" The new orchards of the Columbia Basin had changed the whole industry, Colbert said, because those growers, with the advantage of deep soil and plenty of water and sun, could switch to new varieties of apples in a relatively short time and keep up with ever-shifting consumer tastes.[14]

A.E. VanWinkle, a vice president of the Spokane Bank for Cooperatives, had kept track of Tree Top for almost 20 years, attending its board meetings and giving advice on financial matters. In 1981 he recorded his seasoned observations in an interview. Assessing the cooperative's role, VanWinkle said that if Tree Top had not come along, the whole industry would be "up to our armpits in apples... with no place to market them." An outstanding problem Tree Top had to settle, the banker pointed out, was whether its mission mandated taking all the processing fruit it could get from members and nonmembers alike, which had been the policy in the past, or whether it should firm up membership loyalty, restrict the enrollment, and take only what its grower-owners had to offer. Other agricultural cooperatives, VanWinkle said, dealt only with their own members. In fact, Tree Top continued to struggle for years with the challenging problem of limiting membership and member loyalty.

Other questions facing the Selah-based cooperative, VanWinkle observed, included whether to go nationwide or stay with its well-established regional markets, and whether to make "private label" products for another company, thereby departing from Bill Charbonneau's stubborn determination against doing so. As for a resolution of these two issues, the first one was found, for the time being, in the disappointing march into New York City. The second issue would eventually be settled by several agreements to process goods for distribution under other company labels.

The officers of the Bank for Cooperatives, VanWinkle commented, had worked with Tree Top since the loan to buy out Charbonneau's contract, and they were proud of the cooperative's accomplishments. Because of rapid expansion, Tree Top was "spread pretty thin," but its management realized the need for long-term planning, and the Spokane bankers were pleased to offer their consultation in this "forward thinking." Altogether, Tree Top's first 20 years were a resounding "success story," VanWinkle said, and one that was gratifying to recall. Not only had Charbonneau's insistence on high quality been maintained, but his emphasis on getting and keeping markets had usually prevailed as well.

The retirement of Ernest L. "Ernie" Stafford, veteran director of sales and marketing, signified the passing of an era for Tree Top. Stafford was a connecting link between Charbonneau's private company and the grower-owner cooperative. He had started as Charbonneau's national sales manager in 1955, continued in that capacity, and served as assistant general manager as well as interim general manager. When frozen concentrate was put on sale, he had opened the eastern and southern markets for it, and also initiated promotional programs for the cooperative's expanded product line that had reached into 41 states,

including Alaska and Hawaii. By the time he left in 1974, Ernie Stafford had played a major role in making the Tree Top brand name typify apple juice itself. In retirement, Stafford wrote a valuable history covering the Charbonneau and cooperative periods, from the 1950s into the 1970s.[15]

On a sad note, in 1978, outgoing board chair Ray O'Neal reported that Bill Charbonneau had died during the year. Tree Top would "stand as a living memorial," O'Neal predicted, to the founder's far-reaching achievement of creating "a home" for Washington's once-scorned cull apples. 🍎

Endnotes

1. One early inquiry that suggested the commercial opportunities for marketing evaporated apples may be found in J.S. Caldwell, "Evaporation of Apples," Bulletin 131, Agricultural Experiment Station, State College of Washington, May 1916.
2. See Tawfix Y. Sharkasi, "Dilution and Solids Adulteration of Apple Juice," M.S. thesis, Washington State University, 1979.
3. *Hunt v. Washington State Apple Advertising Commission* 432 U.S. 333 (1977).
4. For the possible advantages of combined cooperative-corporate distribution systems, see W. Smith Greig and Leroy L. Blakeslee, "Potentials for Apple Juice Processing in the U.S. with Implications for Washington," Bulletin 808, College of Agriculture Research Center, Washington State University, Pullman, April 1975.
5. Quotations in this section are from *Tree Topics*, February 1981.
6. For comparative truck and rail shipping rates, as of 1969, from Yakima and various other apple-growing regions to New York City, see W. Smith Greig, "Location Advantages in Applesauce Processing in the U.S. with Some Implications for the Washington Apple Industry," Bulletin 753, Washington Agricultural Experiment Station, Washington State University, 1972, 6. This study also makes comparisons of production costs, population of market areas, and other competitive factors.
7. At this time Tree Top's permanent labor force stood at 250, but rose to 750 in the busy season. The 1976 calendar-year payroll was $3.5 million.
8. Besides Pillsbury, by the early 1980s, Tree Top had to compete in the juice market with several other big private corporations and established processors such as General Mills, Campbell Soup, Mott's (a subsidiary of Cadbury-Schweppes), Minute Maid (a subsidiary of Coca-Cola), Ocean Spray, Seneca, Welch, and Sunsweet.
9. Interim General Manager Dennis Colleran, quoted in *Tree Topics*, November 1982. This issue contains the information presented at the 1982 annual meeting.
10. Although often overlooked, the addition of concentrate could also quickly, and easily, balance the acid level in the blending of juices. At that time the Red Delicious variety, which had low acidity, constituted the great majority of apples grown in Washington and those delivered to Tree Top.
11. The circumstances surrounding the board's pledge are described in the *American/Western Fruit Grower*, September 1983.

12. Although Ward's project of buying foreign concentrate to stabilize the flow of raw product failed in the end, it had helped give temporary support to the rapidly growing cooperative before two successive, overwhelming bumper crops changed all calculations.

13. *Prosser Record-Bulletin*, June 28, 1979.

14. *Tree Topics,* December 1978, December 1981.

15. *Tree Topics*, March 1974. Although Stafford's name is not listed as the author, in the ca. 1970s he undoubtedly wrote the typewritten manuscript, "Tree Top—The Story of Apple Juice," currently deposited in the Tree Top Historical Files.

Top Harvest
BRAND

PURE Apple Juice
NO SUGAR ADDED

K

TREE TOP INC.
SELAH, WASH. 98942
PRODUCT OF U.S.A.

NET 46 FL. OZ. (1 QT. 14 OZ.)

Bottle label for a new product line introduced in the early 1980s.

Chapter 4

The Alar Crisis

Driven by the mission of providing more marketing opportunities and maximum profits for the grower-members, Tree Top's pace of expansion and diversification quickened from the early 1980s into the 1990s. The demand for ingredients by food manufacturers resulted in the formation of a separate industrial division. In the 1960s, apple juice had only been a specialty item, but life-style changes of the 1970s relating to health and nutrition concerns had helped create a booming marketplace. Now the beverage business had become so attractive that more giant national and international conglomerates were crowding into the field, tightening the competitive race, particularly in the western United States. Among the foreign competitors, Chile, China, and Italy joined Argentina by entering U.S. markets, offering juices as well as industrial ingredients. Some of these firms enjoyed government subsidies and advantageous monetary exchange rates. Moreover, with the popularity of various imitation juices rising to challenge the real thing, Tree Top faced the prospect that consumers might forget brand loyalty, which guaranteed high quality and genuine taste, and choose instead cheaper beverages.

On the international scene, the importance of export markets, only tentatively explored in the past, now became a top priority. The cooperative worked out a major co-packing arrangement with Japan and reached out for sales to other parts of the world as well. In short, Tree Top aspired to have a significant role in international trade to match its ambitions in the United States. And by the 1990s, as one sage observed, the firm had assumed the configuration of a three-legged stool. Bottled apple juice alone no longer had to hold up the whole structure; there were two other strong supporting legs, dehydrated products and concentrate.

At home, Tree Top could not escape the issues involved in national social and economic trends. For example, what effect, if any, would the increasing number of single par-

ent families have on the consumption of fruit juices? The depressed economy, lingering inflation, and high interest rates of the early 1980s hit the West especially hard. These problems called for a new marketing program that featured television advertising and promotional coupons, but focused almost exclusively on the most profitable items. In 1985, the cooperative once more restructured its capitalization base with a new equity system for its members that helped stabilize the financial foundation and provide the cash flow for expansion. This important step, again taken with the help of the Spokane Bank for Cooperatives, reconfigured the previous financial overhaul of the late 1970s and was, in part, expedited by the national economic situation. By far the most distressing dilemma, however, came in the raucous public controversy over the use of the fruit spray Alar and the validity of claims that it caused cancer. Even though the cooperative had carefully monitored fruit delivered by the grower-members and segregated the Alar-treated apples into a separate pool, it was hit by the devastating effects suffered by the entire apple industry. Tree Top eventually worked through all of these difficulties, made the necessary adjustments, and continued the highly competitive struggle in the food industry.

The change in executive leadership had little noticeable effect on Tree Top's fast-paced growth. In fact, operations picked up speed under the guidance of Dennis J. Colleran, who emphasized expansion of foreign and domestic markets, additional co-packing arrangements in other states and foreign countries, and the acquisition of competing companies. In other words, as described briefly, he was "into mergers and acqui-

Dennis Colleran.

sitions." First hired as controller in 1971, and made vice president of finance in 1980, Colleran had a background in accounting, having served in executive positions with Price Waterhouse as well as Seattle University and a large private corporation in Seattle. In October 1982, the board of directors appointed him interim president and general manager, and named him CEO that December.

Colleran grew up in the Yakima area, at Prosser, and had a long-time, firsthand understanding of the fruit industry. Known for his exceptional communication skills, he could speak with ease before the Tree Top directors or, dressed in a casual sweater and slacks, he could charm a gathering of orchardists in the Okanogan country. Colleran set the tone of his tenure, even as interim president, with long articles in the company publication *Tree Topics*, explaining in detail his seasoned understanding of the cooperative's problems and the challenges facing the grower-members. His informational articles continued to appear in subsequent issues. As a polished public speaker, he was frequently invited to address regional and national agricultural meetings. These speeches often included Colleran's analyses of broad economic issues affecting worldwide agricultural production and marketing.

For the benefit of the cooperative membership, Colleran explained his leadership philosophy in sports terminology. He recalled his years as coach of a youth basketball team and how difficult it was to stand on the sidelines and let the boys play the game. "I wanted to grab that ball and play the game my way," he said, "but that isn't the job of a coach." He compared Tree Top to a "processing team" with specified rules for the game, assuring the growers that his management group would welcome their suggestions, guidance, and even criticism. "We will play the game with all the skill and ability we possess," Colleran declared, and then cautioned the members that, by the rules of this game, their coaching role restricted them to the sidelines. Of course, although he failed to mention it, coaches always had the power to bench even a star player.

Early on, Colleran also addressed the growers on the sensitive subject of concentrates generally and foreign concentrates specifically. The "changing and turbulent times" of the 1980s, he told them, called for innovative think-

Bob Dennis.

ing. According to Colleran, the cooperative had stopped using foreign concentrate in 1980 because of the growers' protests. The increasingly heavy competition of the juice field, however, placed Tree Top at a disadvantage. While the cooperative, by the nature of its democratic structure, had to depend largely on the members to furnish processor apples for a supply of raw material, the giant rival conglomerates utilized lower-priced concentrates purchased on the world market.

For Tree Top to keep a viable marketing position, Colleran pointed out, it had to introduce new products that catered to changing consumer demands and implement costly promotional programs that strengthened brand loyalty. In doing so, the Selah-based firm lacked the resources for the multi-million-dollar advertising campaigns conducted by big private corporations. As one alternative, it introduced a new product line, bearing the label "Top Harvest," which sold at a more competitive price. In addition, the completion of the Cashmere plant's large bulk tanks for locally produced concentrate would add some stability to the supply pipeline from season to season, and thus help fight off the challenge of those competitors that used foreign concentrates exclusively.

The handwriting was on the wall; foreign concentrates would continue to cause difficulties for Tree Top management. For example, in 1983 some growers had earned $111 a ton for their fruit, but the cash market subsequently dropped to $50 or $60 a ton because of the sizable increase of imported concentrates. Furthermore, the producers using only this source had already captured half of the U.S. juice market, and the volume of foreign imports was steadily growing. Another member of the management team, Vice President of Field Services Robert M. Dennis, placed the situation in its global framework. He carefully explained to the grower-members that a dramatic worldwide increase of apple production would create a large surplus on the international market. Much of this surplus might be converted into concentrate, and a significant part of it imported and used by Tree Top's competitors, thus adversely affecting the firm's profits. Clearly, the Selah-based cooperative no longer functioned solely in a local, regional, and national environment, but on the world scene as well.

Sometime in the not-too-distant future, Tree Top, then the world's largest processor of apples, which were largely supplied by its grower-owners, would have to make a decision on its own utilization of foreign concentrates. CEO Colleran was on record as declaring, "If necessary, we will purchase concentrate when our growers' raw supply is not adequate."[1] But how could management explain the necessity of such purchases when many of the members thought foreign concentrates threatened their very livelihood? As stated in the April 1985 *Tree Topics*:

The use of purchased concentrate has become the single most difficult subject for our membership to understand. That communication difficulty is wrapped within the complexities of an emerging global farmers' market, further complicated by the intricacies of today's apple juice competition. Added to this are the current frustrations within the entire agricultural network.[2]

The argument that finally won over the members simply emphasized the connection between "profitability" for Tree Top products in a fiercely competitive marketplace and the payoff returned to the growers from the cooperative's earnings. In fact, the management team began relying on such off-shore purchases to build new markets, and welcomed periodic big apple crops at home to help sustain these ventures.

This approach seemed like the final solution in bringing stabilization to the raw material pipeline and to Tree Top operations generally. But what if apple crops worldwide experienced a bad year, thereby creating a shortage of off-shore concentrates, as happened in 1990? And what if Washington had a bumper crop that season, but the total national yield registered a shortfall, as also occurred? Actually, this particular national and international situation doubled the price paid for juice apples to Tree Top grower-members, but the weakened American dollar and the sharp rise of energy costs decreased the cooperative's profits significantly, resulting in hasty operational adjustments. Such complications became commonplace for the Selah-based firm as a player on the world scene.

As just indicated, limited financial resources sometimes hampered deals for new acquisitions, the advertising of additional products, or a promotional campaign for fresh markets, but there were ways to solve this. In tandem with the Tree Top board and officers of the Spokane Bank for Cooperatives, Colleran took command in the difficult task of revamping the firm's basic financial structure by over-

hauling the grower equity system. Also, besides the Spokane bank's loans, another source of borrowed funds was now becoming important. Tree Top's own Grower Demand Deposit Account, like a savings bank, gave members the opportunity to invest their money at 1980s interest rates ranging from 6 to 14¼ percent compounded monthly.[3] The attractions of this savings system got special attention in every issue of *Tree Topics* and in other company communications.

In February 1987, board chairman Peter Van Well assessed the most challenging issues Tree Top had faced in the last few years. Without hesitation, Van Well declared, a new equity system had been the toughest single issue the board had wrestled with lately. The challenge came in formulating the best program that would meet both the pressing financial needs of the firm and treat the members fairly. Because of the cooperative's democratic structure, it was a monumental task to convince an estimated 3,500 grower-owners to accept any complicated change that affected their income. The then-current Base Capital Plan that originated in the 1978–79 crop year had eliminated different overhead tonnage charges for some members, which varied with the year of delivery. It had made the initial overhead amount the same for everyone and the total compensation dependent on the volume of fruit processed for the individual. But this plan had also steadily increased the mandatory yearly equity investment per ton, which many orchardists resented.

Under the new system, adopted in 1985 with a major modification in 1994, growers received their earnings in two ways. On delivery they received "Commercial Market Value" for their processing fruit, usually in cash, and at year's end a share of the cooperative's seasonal profits.[4] The innovative separation of compensation into early and later payoffs provided an obvious measurement of both "profitability" and the annual performance of Tree Top's management team in obtaining it. For working capital, the board of directors established a refundable "Withhold" surcharge per ton. In those years when the firm had special funding needs, however, the growers received a combination of cash and refundable, non-interest-bearing "Allocation Certificates," which represented deferred earnings. This means of funding was used as late as 1991. After the last certificates were redeemed in 2001, profits from the sales of nonmember products fulfilled the equity, or operational, needs.

The most important part of the new financial structure, "Base Capital/Market Rights," was the investment, or "equity," the members had to purchase in the cooperative so they could deliver and earn profits on a certain number of tons. These rights, covering both apples and pears but at different rates, also guaranteed members that Tree Top would accept all of their qualifying fruit. Over the years this guarantee, which involved whether or not Tree Top would be a full-service processor without any limit on tonnages delivered, drew a great deal of attention as well as considerable criticism.

The new financial plan had undergone 18 months of research, review, and revisions before the board of directors implemented it on August 1, 1985. In a nutshell, the final version provided funds for expanded production and marketing operations, without placing a heavy burden on the membership. It also pressured CEO Colleran and his management team to make additional profits. For the growers, the program promised a guaranteed market with competitive prices, a reasonable allotment for the cooperative's operational expenses, and long-term value of their refundable Market Rights and Allocation Certificates. The new system worked reasonably well and was not modified substantially until 1994, with the introduction of an easier procedure for acquiring Market Rights and a simplified way of paying for the required equity investment in the firm. Such achievements as the overhaul of the grower equity program, although involving the efforts of many persons, occurred during Dennis Colleran's watch and under his leadership, and he deserved a lion's share of the credit for revolutionizing Tree Top's basic financial structure.

As luck would have it, however, the initiation of the original program in the 1985–86 season, when Tree Top had the capacity to handle bumper crops, coincided with one of the smallest fruit harvests in years. The old dilemma of a pinched raw product supply from the membership caused workforce and salary reductions, a reduced advertising budget, and other painful adjustments. Despite "playing against a stacked deck in the most challenging of its 26 years," [5] the cooperative paid increased returns to its growers, most notably doubling the payments for pears.

In a highly competitive world, Colleran firmly believed that Tree Top had to grow or die. And he was determined not to take the blame for a funeral. If the acquisition of other companies during Colleran's tenure was any indication of its basic health, the cooperative certainly would avoid any last rites in the immediate future. All of the standing facilities had been essentially rebuilt and re-equipped by 1986, starting with the fire-ridden Wenatchee plant in 1975. An addition to the corporate office building in Selah was constructed in 1984. A tempting opportunity in the frozen products line arose when the American Conserving Company in Seattle faced bankruptcy. After a convincing presentation by Colleran, the board authorized buying the failing firm, moved its freezing facility to Wenatchee, and soon started turning out frozen apple slices from this equipment.

The management team and the board also discussed building a bottling plant in Louisiana and a bottling and distribution center in the Southeast, but in both cases delayed taking action for the time being. California was another matter since the Los Angeles area offered the biggest single marketplace in the West. To satisfy the production demands of bustling Southern California, Tree Top based a bottling facility at City of Commerce in 1987. Later the cooperative would establish its own bottling plant at Rialto.

At last, also in 1987, Tree Top achieved the milestone of acquiring the Valley Evaporating Company at Cowiche. Earlier the board of directors had rejected overtures to purchase this historic producer of dried apples, as well as vegetables and berries. In the present surge of expansion, however, that previous reluctance had faded away and the time seemed right to absorb Evap. For three generations, George Hallauer and his family had operated Evap's dried apple facilities in the East before moving to the Pacific Northwest where, in 1977, they sold out to a group of Argentine investors. After sustaining financial losses for three years, the Argentineans approached Tree Top about selling their interests. By this time, most of the company's production activities had been moved to a plant at Cowiche. Although Tree Top decided to phase out the Cowiche facility, the acquisition of Valley Evap eliminated a dried-apple competitor, provided significant additional sales outlets, and offered the possibility of processing vegetables and berries. Moreover, the takeover of this historic firm added considerable prestige to Tree Top's standing in the fruit industry.

In a classical move of horizontal integration, and a prime example of diversification, Tree Top enrolled a similar kind of cooperative on its roster by absorbing U.S. Grape in August 1988. For the previous 10 years, U.S. Grape, one of several cooperatives whose members grew that fruit in the Yakima Valley, had furnished Tree Top with Concord concentrate for use in both retail and industrial sales. All of that time, the grape organization had made overtures to become the sole source of that concentrate and for an even closer association. The merger with U.S. Grape, besides formalizing a natural alliance, added more apple-processing facilities, since grape pressing usually ended by mid-fall. Immediately after concluding the deal, Tree Top made plans, and drew up designs, for construction of a new grape-processing plant at Sunnyside, Washington.

It was an easy fusion, with the 60 or so grape growers being added to Tree Top membership under similar contractual criteria governing apple and pear orchardists. To indicate the importance of this expansion, the Tree Top directors authorized the addition of an extra seat on the board for three years. After that time, the number of directors would again be 12 instead of 13. A special committee, called the "Grape Advisory Council," selected Al Newhouse of Sunnyside to fill this assignment.[6] The addition of the extra board position, however, was short-lived because of Tree Top's financial crisis and retrenchment in 1989–90. As a result, Newhouse's appointment was brief and largely ceremonial. In fact, his name is listed with the other board directors in the 1989 annual report, but not in the 1990 edition. For reasons that will be explained later, the Sunnyside grape-processing plant was not built and the relationship with the grape growers soon cooled down.

As indicated earlier, the long-awaited completion of a dozen bulk concentrate storage tanks at Cashmere in early 1987 marked another step in Tree Top's calculated efforts to obtain additional production and marketing flexibility. These storage facilities consisted of above-ground tanks enclosed by two large structures, with each container rang-

ing in capacity from 25,000 to 100,000 gallons, or the equivalent of 13,600 barrels. Until now, concentrate had been handled, stored, and shipped in barrels, all of which were labor-intensive. Raw product sent to co-packers and the California plant was now shipped in bulk form instead of barrels, at a considerable reduction in transportation and labor costs. And especially in those years with bumper crops, refrigerated concentrate could be preserved indefinitely and tapped when needed. It was indeed a notable breakthrough for the cooperative.

During this period, Tree Top completed the transition from placing its main emphasis on production to a marketing orientation. The marketplace was constantly changing, with the entry of bigger national and international competitors, and this required the cooperative to become more innovative in its promotional efforts and development of product lines. In the mid-1980s, apple juice and dehydrated apple items accounted for the largest part of sales, which had then reached about $170 million. At the same time that sales increased because of rising consumer demand, however, Tree Top had to ward off new competitors and cope with a shrinking market share. In addition, the small profit margin on apple juice caused a shift of attention instead to the possibilities for the dehydration of juice fruit. These perplexing circumstances called for an imaginative management strategy and a lot of good luck.

Since the scope of Tree Top planning was now global, its co-packing and marketing activities in foreign countries reflected this international outreach. Targeted areas included Asia as well as the Caribbean, Latin America, and parts of Europe. For instance, the cooperative scheduled sizable shipments of apple juice to Bahrain, the Persian Gulf islands, and Riyadh, Saudi Arabia. Representatives from the People's Republic of China visited the Selah facilities in the mid-1980s as part of a swing through the Washington apple country. A tour guide gave assurances that the communist country posed no threat to the Evergreen State's fruit industry. "They are a long way from developing an apple industry like Washington's," he said, and continued: "To start with, they don't even have any semi trucks." Friction with China because of its massive injection of concentrate into foreign trade still lay a decade in the future. By that time, China had become the world's number one apple grower.

In the case of Mexico, Tree Top shared its technology with a plant there, expecting to obtain significant amounts of high-acid concentrate. This overture failed to pan out, but Mexico later became one of the most profitable international markets for direct apple juice sales. Management sank several hundred thousand dollars into a risky, speculative, development project in Turkey, hoping for a cheap source of foreign concentrate. After a brief trip to that country, a delegation including two top executives, Robert M. Dennis of field services and LeRoy W. Fletcher of operations, returned with negative reports on the prospects of high-quality concentrate production in Turkey. The whole enterprise soon fizzled after Dennis and Fletcher presented their firsthand observations and the board of directors became fully apprised about the project. Since Yugoslavia also seemed to have some possibilities, CEO Colleran assigned one member of the management team, James M. Sackmann, to study a Slavic language. These instances are representative of Tree Top's interest in foreign countries, but the best example involved co-packing with Japan.

In the late 1980s Tree Top made several co-packing agreements with various Japanese beverage companies, particularly the Pokka firm. To lay the groundwork, Colleran and two other cooperative executives, Andrew J. Murray and Michael Doherty—accompanied by their wives—visited a series of Japanese trade shows. The Americans were jealously shepherded by Pokka International officials, who seemed to want exclusive access to the party. This introduction led to co-packing for Pokka and the other biggest Japanese beverage firms. Strangely enough, because of the high price of aluminum, it was cheaper to co-pack the canned, blended fruit juice in the United States at Selah and ship it to Japanese distributors bearing their labels. Colleran also planned to test-market pure apple juice for sale in Japan, where the main retail outlet for such products was vending machines. Previously, for about three years, Tree Top had shipped to Japan limited amounts of bulk concentrate as well as industrial ingredients. [7]

Dedicated to the strictest of standards, the Japanese firms demanded nothing short of perfection, paying close attention to the slightest deviation in the juice itself as well as the appearance of the cans and packaging. Finally, however, Tree Top became the first U.S. juice and beverage concern to win permission to display on its products the official government symbol of approval. This recognition—the Japanese Agricultural Standards seal (roughly equivalent to the U.S. Good Housekeeping Seal of Approval)—greatly enhanced sales in that Asian country. To obtain this coveted status, Tree Top was required to send six of its employees to a Japanese government training course and to permit ongoing quality inspections. [8]

During these joint activities, Japanese representatives came to the Selah headquarters and established an office nearby in a mobile unit. Meticulously monitoring plant production, these representatives relished long meetings with cooperative personnel where certain equipment and processing procedures were diagramed and discussed at length. At least two Tree Top managers, Ray Hager and Russell Jones, were sent to Japan for extended stays. Hager worked with production operators in the Asahi Soft Drinks Company plant, while Jones did consulting on quality concerns at various facilities. Tree Top spent more than $5 million in remodeling a warehouse at Selah to accommodate the production operations of the special canning process. Sales to all the Pacific Rim countries, but largely to Japan, increased impressively at this time, starting at an insignificant amount in 1987 and registering $24 million by 1989.

In the end, the dollar-yen exchange rate became so unfavorable that the Japanese insisted on changing the marketing agreements, which sharply restricted the cross-ocean exchanges. Also, the facilities in Japan had grown enough to handle its own processing load. By the summer of 1993, Tree Top's export trade with Japan had plunged in one year from $20 million to $13 million, but it was still alive. Two years later, Japanese baking concerns had started relying on local orchards and Chinese apples for most of their fruit ingredients. [9]

Like Hager and Jones, however, most Tree Top managers and executives seemed to agree that this international connection had confirmed, and reinforced, Tree Top's dedication to high quality. In fact, the cooperative probably started a general training program on enhancement of processing operations and quality objectives, called Statical

Process Control, at least in part as a result of the association with the Japanese. In November 1993, NBC News gave recognition to Tree Top's promotion of trade with the Far East, mainly Japan but also China, in a television segment filmed at Selah for airing on an evening news program.[10]

Joint ventures in the United States lasted longer and contributed a steady stream of profits. Co-packing with Citrus World in Florida was highly successful, bringing a 25 percent increase of sales in the southeastern states in 1982 alone. In addition, this alliance gave Tree Top a leg up on its competitors by providing a conveniently located distribution base for markets in the Caribbean. In the then-current management watchword, this kind of success soon created visions of even greater "profitability" in that distant U.S. region. Far-flung co-packing arrangements in such states as Texas and Michigan, as well as Bridgeton, New Jersey, also offered promising prospects. Especially in the case of Bridgeton, as stated in *Tree Topics*: "The difference between co-packing or not co-packing in the East is having Tree Top 'available' or 'not available' in those markets. The brand would not be available in East Coast markets if there were no co-packing agreements to place the juice on the grocery shelf at a competitive price."[11] Concentrate shipped from the Pacific Northwest, then reconstituted and bottled under co-packing arrangements, permitted Tree Top to become virtually a national brand while economizing on shipping costs.

Long-term planning had been practiced at Tree Top since the departure of Bill Charbonneau. In 1989, a revision of the ongoing Strategic Plan called for an ambitious expansion of the cooperative's operations by establishing a packaging and marketing center in the Southeast. No raw product would be processed in the new facility; concentrate from the members' tonnages would be transported from the Pacific Northwest. The proposed venture, envisioned as a preemptive location advantage for the Selah-based firm over its powerful but geographically restricted competitors, would also bolster Tree Top's national image. That project had to be tabled because of intervening disruptive events, as explained later in this chapter, and not because of faltering second thoughts or an alteration of the expansive master plan. As the record shows, the southeastern center, although aborted, characterized the management team's enterprising goals at that time. The co-packing agreement with Florida's Citrus World continued to prove worthwhile,

as did a string of similar joint arrangements stretching out from Texas to Michigan to New York state, all strategically positioned to tap the major urban centers as retail juice markets.

As always, the addition of new markets and untried products depended largely on the raw material pipeline in a given year. In this context a new determining factor caused a great deal of uncertainty, beginning in the early 1980s. Between 1978 and 1982, the Washington state apple industry saw a tremendous increase in the planting of new trees, most notably in the Columbia Basin area straddling the Columbia River.[12] Much of the part east of the Columbia had been covered with sagebrush until irrigation water from Grand Coulee Dam arrived in the 1950s. Two decades later apple orchards became a local "hot commodity." The new "high-density plantings" of the Columbia Basin were on virgin ground, and would bear fruit "in an unbelievably short growing time of three to four years." As these orchards began maturing, Tree Top management wondered aloud about "the tremendous effect" this phenomenon would have on processing, and the entire fruit industry itself. True, significantly larger crops should mean significantly more culls for processing. But how much more, and what extra bank loans for new facilities and equipment would be required to handle the additional load? In short, how could dependable planning be made with the old rules thrown out the window?

The effects in statistics were soon revealed. In 1978, the estimated total of apple orchards in Washington was 115,000 acres, while by 1986 it was probably 168,000 acres, with a significant part of the increase presumably in the Columbia Basin. Between 1977 and 1987, apple production doubled in Washington. Then, in 1987, came "the granddaddy" of all bumper crops—the legendary harvest that for years would be regarded as a benchmark. Strangely enough, the huge crop of 1987 drew cries of despair from the apple industry because of a glutted market and plummeting prices. For Tree Top, the bumper harvest of 1987, and a record crop in 1989, satisfied the cooperative's current processing needs, but, because of depressed prices and competitive factors, failed to bring the big payments expected by the members. In the vicious raw-product cycle, however, short worldwide harvests in 1990 and 1991 stimulated a renewed urgency to plant even more trees.

Early on, it became apparent that too many trees were being planted. Tax breaks for absentee owners had encouraged "investor-type people" (e.g., doctors, lawyers, and those with inherited wealth) to put their money into the big, new orchards of the Columbia Basin and elsewhere in eastern Washington. In fact, big sections of older orchards in the Yakima and Wenatchee valleys, with a low-density per acre of larger trees, were replaced by new, high-density plantings of semi-dwarf or dwarf varieties. Regardless, a revision of the tax code ended the advantages for "the big city investors," who pulled their money out, but left behind the enlarged orchard acreages and prospects of a continuing surplus of fruit.[13] In the end, the industry had to accommodate a tremendous increase of fruit. For its part, the Selah-based cooperative simply offered membership to the new growers and folded their crops into the firm's burgeoning enterprises. Fortunately, because of the timely expansion of facilities and acquisition of other firms, Tree Top was "ahead of the curve" when the big increase of crops came in, and could handle its share.

Meanwhile, the relentless demand to provide new products and maximum profits for the membership continued to claim center stage. New corporate and institutional customers included airlines, convenience stores, vending machines, restaurants and fast food concerns (most notably McDonald's), and similar outlets. Tree Top's management took a great deal of pride in supplying ingredients for Gerber's baby foods and equal satisfaction in a service agreement with Disneyland. Bonnie Peterson, director of New Product Development, spearheaded such projects as the amusement park enterprise. At Disneyland, Mickey and Minnie Mouse characters as well as Johnny Appleseed introduced the cooperative's hot and cold apple cider, as well as sparkling and regular apple juice at the "Juice Wagon," located at the entrance of a new theme attraction called Big Thunder Ranch. It was estimated that 12 million visitors would pass by that spot annually. Available at several other stops in the

Bonnie Peterson.

amusement park, Tree Top became the official apple juice of Disneyland. Another promising outlet for juices, known as special markets, included most ships of the U.S. Navy and military commissaries and post exchanges at American bases around the world. Significantly, by the mid-1980s, the rapidly expanding industrial ingredients market accounted for 17 percent of Tree Top's total sales amounting to $180 million.

The Research and Development division had a new building with the most modern laboratory equipment. Led by Dr. H. Wallace Ewart and other scientists with specialized graduate degrees, the R&D staff labored at the development and testing of additional marketable products. In

collaboration with sales and promotional personnel, the researchers spent two years looking for a profitable, mainline outlet for pear concentrate. The result was a product line of juices called "Rainbow Blends," which featured "Fruit n' Apple," "Fruit n' Grape," and similar combinations based on pear concentrate. By special arrangement, western Washington growers contracted their raspberries for a "Fruit n' Berry" drink that quickly became the most popular choice among these blends. Television advertising, under the theme "Tree Top Your Day," was the most expensive yet for a new product line. But such a formidable introduction was considered necessary if the cooperative hoped to get into the multi-billion-dollar world of specialized fruit drinks. Initial marketing results for these blends confirmed that the cooperative had the capacity to absorb bumper pear crops predicted for the years ahead.[14]

With all the attempts to develop new items, a few flops were inevitable. A large drier tower was constructed at Cashmere to produce apple fiber. Since the fiber had dietary properties like bran, it supposedly would be welcomed for commercial use in food items, bakery goods, and even in pharmaceuticals and cosmetic applications. R&D also successfully tested a high-fiber dietary drink in several flavors called Fiber Rich. The trouble was that the huge drier facility never worked dependably, so this expensive project was eventually called off. Another miscalculation was Stickered Apples (fresh, wrapped apples bearing the Washington state logo and a Tree Top "sticker," or label), whose failure, nevertheless, did not jinx the introduction of such products as fresh Flat Fruit and Frozen Juice Bars in retail sales or frozen slices for the industrial market. Then there was Rockertz, or apple sauce in a plastic tube, that was aimed at the juvenile market, but it apparently never caught on among kids.

With limited funding for promotional campaigns, Tree Top often developed new products aimed at a "niche," or specialty lineup, in the marketplace. The familiar, and dependable, "Tree Top" trademark had helped secure favored recognition on grocery store shelves for the cooperative's apple juice, blends, and apple sauce, and in the wider world, for its industrial ingredients. As an example of this focus, Tree Top manufactured a mixed fruit concentrate, based on pears, to meet the special demands of the baking industry for a strong, naturally flavored sweetener to use along with, or instead of, refined sweeteners.

In 1987, board members Marvin Jeffries and John Clayton got firsthand exposure to another form of the niche "marketing game" by visiting on-site with Tree Top brokers and buyers in the Los Angeles and Phoenix areas. Tours of several supermarkets revealed the importance of advantageous shelf location, attractive packaging, and aisle-end displays. As always, gaining or losing shelf space became a matter of life and death for any wholesaler. "Losing shelf space is the most dangerous thing a company can do," Clayton observed, adding that it was usually determined by "whatever price concessions and promotions a company is willing to give to the retailer in exchange for getting shelf space for their product." As emphasized previously, the problem for Tree Top sometimes came down to whether

the raw material pipeline would support the shelf space waiting to be stocked.

Creative advertising matched the changing times. In a series of publicity overhauls, Tree Top launched a bonus program in early 1983, as the first in a series of promotions described on its product labels. The customer was offered a free cookbook, a discount coupon for the next purchase, and a complimentary copy of a leading health and fitness magazine. In late 1986, a revamped advertising campaign targeted "America's fickle consumer," delivering dire warnings about imitation fruit drinks. The theme—"Tree Top. We Always Give You 100%"—once more emphasized dietary concerns and the cooperative's "good for you" reputation. Companion ads and television commercials went head to head with those competitors who used sugar or corn syrup sweeteners, pointedly specifying corporate names.

In addition, the cooperative continued its utilization of the "Coupon Craze" by distributing them in grocery stores and newspapers. A later program capitalized on the "Wave" (a sequence of stand-up cheers at sporting events),

which kicked off with a Tree Top coupon offer printed on 35 million boxes of Kellogg's cereals, some varieties of which contained ingredients furnished by the cooperative. Another promotion emphasized the theme "Taste the Difference," which, through broad-based advertising, assured the mother with young children "that she can put her trust in Tree Top and its growers." Special ads that also appealed to women appeared in appropriate magazines, such as *Family Circle* and *Good Housekeeping*, and, as recognition of the rapidly increasing Hispanic population, there were ads in Spanish.

No detail was overlooked, it seemed. Not surprisingly, in August 1987, Tree Top decided to "retire the marching letters," that is, to replace the old lettering on the labels with a more eye-catching style. The Landor design firm of San Francisco, which listed several prestigious clients including Coca-Cola, was hired and began extensive research in four large cities. Customer recognition of the cooperative's image, it was found, came from the vivid fresh apple depicted on the label, not from the marching letters, which, in fact, seemed to suggest a "'just for kids'" product. Moreover, grocery buyers not only gave Tree Top apple juice a premium rating, they also associated its celebrated reputation with a visual image of the color green on the present label.

It was a real challenge to create a design that would attract the customer in four seconds, reportedly the average time it took to recognize a product and decide to buy it. The final format was chosen from among 500 lettering styles because it preserved the "contemporary nostalgic appearance" of the original, as well as "a lot of the warmth and country feel" that had made Tree Top successful. [15] The new label featured a striking green color, a bright red apple, and a stated guarantee of 100 percent fruit purity for the individual juice or blend. Interestingly, this alteration of the logo became, in the process, an examination of Tree Top's "public image" and its own self-perception.

It was fortunate that Tree Top had this opportunity to assess its fundamental character because the Selah-based firm soon encountered the greatest crisis it would ever face. In fact, the "Alar scare" of 1989 brought Tree Top to serious financial stress. Known by scientists as daminozide, the chemical was sold as a spray under the trade name Alar. It was widely used in orchards to keep apples appreciably longer on the tree; improve color, size, and shape; and enhance storage life. The potentially dangerous properties of daminozide could not be washed off, eliminated by peeling, or removed by even the most thorough processing. A nonprofit public watchdog, the Natural Resources Defense Council (NRDC), became concerned about research claiming that Alar's chemical properties produced a cancer-causing carcinogen in laboratory animals. As a result, the organization issued a controversial report predicting that 6,000 children might develop cancer from ingesting daminozide in food products. And the report specified apples treated with Alar.

In response, one government official gloomily observed, "Apples, cancer and children—it was all people had to see." [16] Apple juice and other apple items immediately disappeared from home refrigerators and school menus alike. Dissatisfied with the federal Environmental Protection Agency's action on the matter, NRDC made the uncharacteristic decision of hiring a public relations agency to spread its side of the story. The subsequent intense media campaign hit the bull's eye.

On February 26, 1989, the popular Sunday evening CBS television program *60 Minutes* ran the first of two segments apprising 40 million viewers of the distinct possibility that Alar caused cancer. The narrator was the respected investigative reporter Ed Bradley, whose interviews that evening with an NRDC lawyer, the acting director of EPA, and some scientific specialists tended to confirm these suspicions. No reference was made in the commentary to Washington as the leading apple-producer, nor even to "red apples" specifically, but the state's reputation was well known and the accompanying visual images left no doubt about the fruit in question. Bradley's editorial comments were especially damaging to Tree Top: "Kids are at high risk from…[Alar's chemical properties] because they drink so much apple juice. The average preschooler drinks 18 times more apple juice than his or her mother. If those apples are treated with daminozide, the cancer risk is perilously high." [17] And that was only the beginning of the damage.

The media coverage of the Alar scare blossomed as *60 Minutes* ran a follow-up segment that introduced Bradley next to a red apple and skull and crossbones symbol displayed on the screen. One of *Time* magazine's covers showed an apple with a forbidding slash mark across it, and another cover depicted various food items, including two clearly distinguishable Red Delicious apples, with the disturbing question, "Is Anything Safe?" The cover of *Newsweek* portrayed a shopping bag full of vegetables and fruit, including a red apple, with "DANGER" stamped at the top of the bag, and asking, "How Safe Is Your Food?"[18] The visual images of Red Delicious apples in connection with Alar and cancer, as portrayed in the *60 Minutes* segments and numerous other widely circulated venues such as *Time* and *Newsweek*, undoubtedly contributed to the decline in popularity of that variety. Since that time, when Red Delicious made up 80 percent of the crop in Washington state, that apple variety's share has dropped to about 30 percent. In fact, a popular saying of that day held out the dire prediction that "Red is Dead," which proved to be only a slight exaggeration.

Daytime network television shows, such as *Today* on NBC and *Good Morning America* on ABC, aired several Alar stories, as did the evening newscasts. Countless newspapers and magazine articles dwelt on the subject, and media outlets around the world spread the bad news. Probably the most telling blows were delivered by the famous actress Meryl Streep, who, beginning with a television appearance on the *Phil Donahue Show* and followed by several other media forays, became the crusading spokesperson against Alar. A celebrity mother of three, she emphasized the cancer-related danger to children, which was the alarming message she also presented in testimony before a congressional subcommittee.[19]

As supermarkets pulled all apple products off their shelves and mothers rejected both apples and apple juice for their kids, a devastating shock wave swept across the fruit industry, costing many growers their orchards and estimated overall losses of $100 million. It was bad enough that schools in New York, Chicago, Los Angeles, and other big cities had banned the fruit in any form from their cafeterias. But when some districts in Washington itself took the same action, it was the last straw.

Despite its best efforts, Tree Top could not escape the fallout. Three years before the crisis, as early warnings surfaced, the cooperative's board had confronted the problem and decided that Alar-treated fruit posed an "unreasonable business risk" and possible legal difficulties. As a result, in 1986 the directors had adopted the policy of not accepting any apples treated with Alar spray in that growing season. The cooperative's publication, *Tree Topics*, apprised the members of the new stance, adding: "A monitoring system

is being established to test apples delivered for the presence of this chemical. Any apples found to contain Alar from recent treatments will be released to the grower, who will be free to dispose of the fruit elsewhere." The members also received a letter with more details.[20]

During the next two years, because of the widespread use of the spray by its membership, Tree Top announced that Alar-treated fruit would be "segregated into a separate pool" and not used in its branded products. On one hand, the Selah-based firm recognized its responsibility to protect consumers; on the other hand, its grower-owners were desperate to find a market for their fruit. On May 10, 1989, just before the second *60 Minutes* segment, the board voted flatly not to accept any more of the chemically sprayed apples for that season. Then, after vociferous protests from the grower ranks, the directors changed that decision. On May 31, the board essentially reiterated the previous policy of a separate pool for deliveries of Alar-treated fruit and hunkered down to ride out the storm. Even with the early installation of a monitoring system, however, it was difficult to thoroughly inspect the thousands of tons of fruit delivered by an estimated 3,500 members.

In March 1989, *Consumer Reports* magazine tested Tree Top products marketed in the New York City area and found some evidence of Alar in those selected samples. The periodical generally concluded that a five-in-a-million risk of cancer existed in eating apples.[21] In comparison, smoking cigarettes had a one-in-three risk of premature death. Infuriated Tree Top members in the Yakima Valley took out their wrath on actress Meryl Streep, saying they had invited her to visit their orchards and processor facilities. Regarding themselves as practicing environmentalists, they wanted Streep to see firsthand how many small family orchardists had been hurt by her comments, and to tell her that their cooperative had banned Alar-treated fruit in its branded products three years before she became a crusader. Streep apparently never responded to their invitation.[22]

Earlier, when the Alar blitz had first hit, the Tree Top directors, as previously indicated, chose a strategy of lying low until effective resolutions could be formulated. Meanwhile, the less said and the less attention drawn to the cooperative's operations, the better. Not so with CEO Dennis Colleran, who decided on a proactive approach to the Alar problem. His strategy included getting into the media with a positive message that would swing public opinion in favor of the apple industry and take "the steam" out of the media attacks.

While the Washington Apple Commission and his own board ducked for cover, Colleran took the initiative in lobbying Congress to ban Alar without delay. He also hired the largest, most prestigious Seattle public relations firm and authorized extensive advertising aimed at informing the general public "of Tree Top's long-standing practice of screening out Alar-treated apples from Tree Top branded products." As a part of this ambitious campaign, expensive ads appeared in nationally prominent newspapers.

Colleran also entered the battle personally in a Seattle speech, and with other public statements. Addressing a luncheon meeting of the Greater Seattle Chamber of Commerce, he declared that Tree Top was "going to do anything we can to get Alar off the market." That the chemical spray had not been "proven guilty by science" made no difference now, Colleran was quoted as saying, because it had "become a huge liability." He sympathized with mothers who thought their children were at risk, and his heart went out to those Washington growers losing their orchards and others who had "suffered terrible losses." Washington apple sales had fallen 25 percent following the first *60 Minutes* broadcast, and estimated industry losses would eventually amount to between $100 and $200 million. Colleran confided to his Seattle audience that Tree Top itself had scaled back estimates of annual sales from an expected $300 million to $260 million. [23]

Colleran's general comments, much less his revelation of in-house information, were the last thing the Tree Top directors wanted to hear at this particular time. From their viewpoint, Colleran's proactive approach, instead of forming favorable public opinion, had created a "lightning rod" that drew unfavorable media attention to Tree Top and other processing firms. His sympathies in the Alar scare seemed to focus too much on general concerns, and not enough on the plight of members in his own cooperative. Angry grumbling in the membership and from associated warehouse managers confirmed this opinion. Consequently, a week after his Seattle talk, the *Seattle Times* announced that Colleran had resigned, "reportedly over his pro-consumer stance on the chemical Alar." No official reason was given, but insiders said that the board had forced him out because of his approach "on handling the Alar controversy." [24]

Undoubtedly, the Alar episode had brought the differences between Colleran and the directors to a head. Probably other factors were of equal influence in his departure, including a strong apprehension among some directors, and many grower-members as well, that the CEO had introduced too much expansion, especially in high-risk international trade projects. Tree Top was simply getting "too big for its britches." For instance, some critics brought up the speculative and expensive endeavor in Turkey that fizzled, as well as the overpriced Japanese venture and other projects with sizable cost overruns. Also, the policy of purchasing foreign concentrate still rankled some influential growers, and others were unhappy with the new equity system.

The bottom line, however, always came back to promised "profitability." For the past two years, the growers had received less than they expected for their fruit—first because of the bumper crop and a glut on the market, and next because of the Alar scare. In light of these financial shortfalls, a special category of complaints focused on the generous bonuses recently received by the management team. The "buck" stopped at the CEO's desk.

It made little difference in Colleran's departure that the Alar controversy produced no generally accepted scientific evidence conclusively proving a high-risk connection between the chemical spray and cancer in humans. Nor did it matter that the manufacturer voluntarily took the chemical off the market. [25] Regardless, Colleran had left an enviable record. When he became CEO, annual sales for 1982 were about $137 million, while the amount for 1989 was more than $276 million. In the 1980–81 season, the cooperative processed 233,480 tons of apples, with returns to the growers of $80 per ton; the comparable figures for 1988 were more than 458,000 tons of apples, grapes, and pears, and returns of between $57 and $107; and for the disastrous Alar year of 1989, nearly 231,000 tons, and payouts of between $33 and $55.

These raw statistics failed to show how much Colleran and his management team had expanded Tree Top's horizons, nor would the compilations indicate his other important contributions, such as overhauling the cooperative's basic capitalization system. But since figures counted for so much, Colleran himself took satisfaction in what he had witnessed during his years at Tree Top. Between 1971, when he was hired as controller, and 1989 when he left as

CEO, annual sales had increased from about $9 million to a volume approaching $300 million. Undoubtedly, Dennis Colleran had played a key role in this remarkable record of growth. 🍎

Endnotes

1. *American/Western Fruit Grower*, September 1983.
2. *Tree Topics*, April 1985.
3. Regarding the sources of the growers' income available for investment, only about 5 percent came from processing fruit, while the other 95 percent derived from sales on the fresh-fruit market. *Tree Topics*, April 1987.
4. Actually, in most cases, the growers delivered their fruit, both for the fresh market and processing, to warehouses, which were paid by Tree Top for deliveries of culls, and which, in turn, paid the orchardists.
5. *Tree Topics*, October 1986.
6. *Tree Topics*, May/June, December, 1988.
7. "Tree Top Deal with Japan to Bring $15 Million in Sales," *Seattle Times,* March 16, 1988, A9.
8. Ibid.
9. *Apple Corps*, Spring 1995.
10. Tree Top served as a pathfinder for the overall Washington state apple industry, penetrating the Japanese market several years before the fresh-apple business did so with limited success. See *Seattle Times* articles: February 19, 1995; Alwyn Scott, "Japan's Import Barriers on U.S. Apples Ruled Illegal," June 23, 2005. See also, Linda Calvin and Barry Krissoff, "Resolution of the U.S.-Japan Apple Dispute: New Opportunities for Trade," Outlook Report No. FTS31801, U.S. Department of Agriculture, Economic Research Service, October 2005. www.ers.usda.gov/Publications/FTS/oct05/FTS31801.
11. *Tree Topics*, May 1986.
12. See A. Desmond O'Rourke, *The Washington Apple Industry to the Year 2000*, Information Series No. 58, IMPACT Center, College of Agriculture and Home Economics, Washington State University, February 1993. This booklet assessed the Washington apple industry from the 1980s to the early 1990s, and made predictions to 2000.
13. Bruce Ramsey, "It's a Bumper Apple Crop—But Farmers Are Still Worried," *Seattle Post-Intelligencer*, September 2, 1987, A1; Bruce Ramsey, "Apple Growers Feel the Squeeze: Record Crop Drives Prices below Production Costs," *Seattle Post-Intelligencer*, February 16, 1988, B5. In the 1980s, Washington state apple harvests increased by 40 percent, and would grow another 27 percent in the first half of the 1990s.
14. Brand loyalty for the firm's "100% Pure Apple Juice," however, remained so strong that the new blends of "Apple Pear," "Apple Raspberry," etc. were soon renamed so that the well-known words "Tree Top" led the way on the labels, thus avoiding confusion among faithful consumers. *Tree Topics*, October/November 1987.
15. *Tree Topics*, August/September 1987.
16. Jim Begnim, Massachusetts Department of Food and Agriculture, quoted in "How Safe Is Your Food?" *Newsweek*, March 27, 1989, 16.
17. *Auvil v. CBS "60 Minutes"* 800 F. Supp. 928 (E.D. Wash. 06/5/1992). The text of this class action suit in the U.S. District Court for the Eastern District of Washington contains the verbatim first segment on Alar of the *60 Minutes* program. Grady Auvil, a well-known Washington orchardist and member of the Tree Top cooperative, led the group of plaintiffs, whose case met with adverse rulings in the federal courts.
18. For samples of the front covers and accompanying articles, see *Time*, "Is Anything Safe?" March 27, 1989, 24–38, and *Newsweek*, "How Safe Is Your Food?" March 27, 1989, 15–23.
19. General accounts of the Alar scare are in online editions of the *Wall Street Journal*, October 3, 1989, and Elliott Negin, "The Alar 'Scare' Was for Real; and So Is that 'Veggie Hate-Crime' Movement," and Letters to the Editor, *Columbia Journalism Review* 35 (September/October 1996) and (November/December 1996). See also: "2 State Schools Take Apples off Menu, for Now," *Seattle Post-Intelligencer*, March 1, 1989, B1; Joel Connelly, "Apples Have Dramatic Role in the Senate," *Seattle Post-Intelligencer*, March 17, 1989, A1.
20. *Tree Topics*, March/April, 1986.
21. "Alar: Not Gone, Not Forgotten," *Consumer Reports* 54, no. 5 (May 1989).
22. The effects of the Alar scare among Yakima Valley apple growers and their invitation to Meryl Streep is presented in Timothy Egan, "Yakima Valley Journal: Farming without Alar, Suffering with the Rest," *New York Times*, March 24, 1989.
23. Bruce Ramsey, "Tree Top Steps Up Alar War," *Seattle Post-Intelligencer*, May 24, 1989, B8; "Prices of Apples Hit New Lows: State Growers near Panic as Alar Scare Slashes Sales by 15%," *Seattle Post-Intelligencer*, May 27, 1989, B3; Bruce Ramsey, "Chief of Tree Top Quits," *Seattle Post-Intelligencer*, June 1, 1989, B7; "Apple Growers at Risk, Executive Says," *Seattle Post-Intelligencer*, May 24, 1989, E10.
24. "Tree Top President Resigns," *Seattle Times*, June 1, 1989, B1; Bruce Ramsey, "Chief of Tree Top Quits," *Seattle Post-Intelligencer*, June 1, 1989, B7
25. See Elliott Negin, "The Alar 'Scare' Was for Real; and So Is that 'Veggie Hate-Crime' Movement," and Letters to the Editor, *Columbia Journalism Review* 35 (September/October 1996) and (November/December 1996). Negin's article and the subsequent letters assess the validity of the Alar threat, and also discuss the counteroffensive financed by agri-business interests. See also for the manufacturer voluntarily stopping Alar sales: Joel Connelly, "Maker of Alar to Voluntarily Halt U.S. Sales," *Seattle Post-Intelligencer*, June 3, 1989, A1. The July 1990 issue of *Consumer Reports* ("No More Bad Apples," 446), stated that Alar had "essentially vanished from the food supply."

TREE TOP
Major U.S. Retail Juice Markets

Seattle

Portland

Minneapolis

Milwaukee

San Francisco
Sacramento

Salt Lake City

Denver

Chicago

Kansas City

Los Angeles

Phoenix

San Diego

Oklahoma City/Tulsa

Dallas
Houston
San Antonio

Tree Topics (January 1994).

Chapter 5

Tree Top and Globalization

The Alar troubles could not have come at a more inopportune time for Tree Top. With finances already strained to the limit, the cooperative had invested heavily on expanding major new markets both overseas and at home. As George Chapman, chair of the board of directors, stated in the 1989 annual report:

These investments could not pay off when the Alar scare flared up. Buyers in the trade, perceiving weakness in consumer confidence, avoided displaying or promoting our products, while demanding low prices that denied us decent profit margins...In short, we were making some major expenditures based on projected growth which did not and could not occur. We had staff in place to accommodate an unrealized sales base. We invested in distribution and promotions which did not materialize. We experienced a sales slowdown while carrying out programs which proved ineffective.

To make matters more problematical, a debt of more than $1 million was owed for advertising, principally on a contract with a Seattle public relations firm that CEO Colleran had hired to offset the unfavorable media blitz in the Alar scare. The cumulative financial crunch caused operating losses and a great deal of dissatisfaction among the growers over reduced earnings.

The main creditor, a Puget Sound area bank, advised what amounted to liquidation of the cooperative, a drastic alternative that Chapman firmly rejected. In Chapman's dinner meeting with bank executives, he had been told that the lending agency had a buyer standing by who was ready to assume Tree Top's debts and take over its operations as a private company. The transaction would include no exchange of money—that is, no payoff to a proposed defunct Tree Top—nor would the grower-owners receive anything for their equity in the cooperative or any assur-

George Chapman.

ance about their delivery rights in the new firm. When the bankers finished, it was clear that the deal would rescue their loans to Tree Top, and nothing more. At this point, Chapman abruptly got up and quickly headed out of the dining room toward the exit, only to be intercepted by the bank executives with a conciliatory and more equitable offer. Tree Top had narrowly escaped being turned over to private ownership.

Not surprisingly, the plan to establish a big distribution center in the southeastern United States was shelved. Likewise, the proposal to build a major grape-processing plant at Sunnyside, contemplated since the merger with U.S. Grape, suffered the same fate. Other elements of the now discarded master blueprint for increased sales, for marketplace dominance, and, generally, for a high profile in the field also fell by the wayside. Instead, "redirective changes" in management focused on the profitable marketing of basic products. In a nutshell, the cooperative was retooled as a somewhat scaled-down model. Whereas the old Tree Top had been "spread too thin in too many directions," the new version would "avoid risks and uncertainty" in the business world.

The changed configuration was reflected in a different slate of managers. Not only was Dennis Colleran gone, but also the names of four out of six other members of the previous management team did not appear on the new roster. [1] Board chair Chapman temporarily filled the gap in executive leadership. A new interim president and CEO, Robert S. Conroy, was hired only until "Troubled Tree Top," as described by a Seattle newspaper, could recruit a permanent leader. An experienced, respected former executive in the food industry, Conroy had served as CEO of Lamb-Weston Inc., which specialized in potato and other vegetable products.[2] He set out immediately to reduce costs, cut back on unnecessary growth, project a lower business profile, and, above all, obtain more "profitability" and greater returns to the growers.

A year later, in the 1990 annual report, board chair George Chapman declared that all of Conroy's main goals had been achieved, and things had "turned out nicely." This did not mean, according to Chapman, that Tree Top had "turned the corner" on all of its difficulties, but instead that the cooperative had "outlived the Alar debacle." The present management, he said, was "smarter about expansion and risk," but, as to its continued success, "the jury is still out." One thing was certain, Chapman warned the grower-owners, there was "no free lunch" for them. The firm's capitalization must be increased, and loyal members, who delivered all their eligible fruit to Tree Top instead of seeking higher prices elsewhere, could easily do the job. Otherwise, the cooperative had little hope for the future in an expanded marketplace where competitors and their budgets were getting bigger and bigger.

CEO Conroy, a methodically efficient executive, also reported on his first year's record of "attempting to lead Tree Top out of the financial and management crisis precipitated by the consumer Alar panic." After detailing his various corrective actions, Conroy announced what sounded like scaled-down but familiar goals of the recent past. "Over the longer term," he said, "new products and [expanded] distribution are essential to maintaining a leadership position." He outlined some of the modest beginnings in that direction, such as improving the apple juice flavor, enhancing the taste of apple sauce, and initiating a program to ensure high quality requirements. In addition, management had made two important joint distribution arrangements, one with a major company noted for penetrating the difficult convenience store and vending machine markets. In the other agreement, the famous Schweppes bottlers would handle a line of Tree Top beverages in the eleven western states. Contractual negotiations were also underway with Pepsico, which produced and distributed snack foods, to introduce apple chips into supermarket chains.

Bob Conroy.

And so, the Alar scare gradually faded away. In 1990, like a formal pronouncement of the conclusion, Tree Top grower-member Grady Auvil and 10 other Washington apple growers filed a lawsuit against CBS, *60 Minutes*, and the Natural Resources Defense Council seeking compensation for lost sales because of "false, misleading, and scientifically unreliable statements." The case went all the way to the U.S. Supreme Court where previous rulings against the growers in the lower courts were upheld. [3] Meanwhile, Tree Top had started the process of pulling itself out of the Alar situation. The Selah-based cooperative had "lost its innocence" in that crisis, and a few years would pass before it regained the lost ground. But it emerged as a leaner, tougher competitor and better prepared to fight for a prominent place in domestic and world markets.

Unlimited expansion had previously been the main objective. Now, as an example of how Tree Top acquired operational funds to continue, the cooperative not only abandoned its plans for building a new grape-processing plant at Sunnyside but sold off the existing facility that it had obtained from U.S. Grape. At the same time, efforts to cut back on expenses included more stringent control of inventories on hand, a reduction in the number of warehouse and shipping locations utilized, and the more timely collection of accounts receivable. [4]

Operating expenses dropped by about $8.6 million. Notable savings had been achieved by reducing inventories throughout the company. Bottom-line improvement of finances also helped jump-start the recovery. Income for fiscal year 1990 increased by $13.8 million over the previous year, making the net loss $5.5 million compared with $8.3 million earlier. Tonnage returns to the apple growers for 1990 inspired even greater optimism. Juice fruit brought about $57, up 71 percent; peelers about $108, up 94 percent; and pears about $35, up 61 percent. The possibility of liquidation, faced and rejected by board chair George Chapman, now seemed remote since the 1990 balance sheet included $16.3 million in cash on hand and short-term investments, as compared with the dangerously low amount of $1.9 million in 1989. Perhaps equally important, the cooperative now had the back-up support of a bank line of credit of up to $70 million. Even with the uncertainties of a nationwide recession, the prospects for continuation of this "positive momentum" appeared to be good. Tree Top was moving forward and could come up for a breath of air.

As Tree Top moved back to its pre-Alar role in the retail marketplace, it soon became apparent that the field had changed. The brief absence of promotional activity had drawn consumer attention away from apple juice to alternative beverages, primarily orange drinks. Accordingly, the consumption of apple juice had declined by double digit percentages in a matter of months. Furthermore, an increase in product prices to pay for needed advertising was especially difficult because of a lingering recession. The subsequent promotional campaign emphasized Tree Top's trademark virtues of high quality and genuine taste with the slogans "Taste the Difference" and "More Fresh Apple Taste." Reports were a little less encouraging on the ingredients side, including domestic industrial sales and international marketing. Locked-in annual contracts for such transactions left no room to increase these prices. Still, the cooperative recorded profits in industrial-international business over returns during the Alar period. Tree Top was back in the big race with a 20 percent market share.

The temporary leadership of Robert S. Conroy ended with the appointment of Frank Elsener as president and CEO in July 1992. As already mentioned, Conroy had accepted the position during the Alar crisis with the agreement that he would stay long enough "to see the company through a major re-focusing of its efforts and clarification of its goals." In January, with Tree Top "stabilized," a search had started for Conroy's successor. With the assistance of a professional executive search organization, Conroy and the Tree Top board determined that Elsener had the background in both domestic and international operations to guide the cooperative in the post-Alar period. Indeed, Elsener's impressive qualifications included 35 years of experience in food production and marketing with such firms as Procter and Gamble, Hunt Wesson, and a large Canadian concern, J.L. LaBatt

Frank Elsener.

Ltd. [5] Significantly, from this time on, relations between the CEOs and the board became much closer and the lines of communication were used more often as well as more effectively.

Elsener came onboard just as the directors reaffirmed the cooperative's mission of serving the grower-members by handling all of their processing fruit. As before, the goals included providing a stable marketing outlet, obtaining higher returns than cash-market rates, and developing new markets. About this time, the Selah-based firm also changed the method of member compensation, offering a choice between Season Average Option, in which earnings were based on the average market value during the entire season regardless of when the fruit was delivered, and Current Market Option, which was calculated on the market price at the specific time of delivery. This latter option allowed the orchardists to hold their fruit, if they chose to do so, and speculate on when to sell it at the best price instead of accepting a seasonal average. [6] Simultaneously a drive was launched to increase membership, which was listed at 3,500 but may have been much smaller. Recruiting invitations went out by mail to 3,500 nonmember growers in Washington, Oregon, and Idaho. The obvious objective in all of these initiatives was to bolster the fluctuating supply pipeline of raw product coming to Tree Top.

Frank Elsener promptly outlined several other management objectives, which were somewhat different from the "aggressive growth strategy" of the pre-Alar period. High on his list was a substantial expansion of the industrial ingredients business, which now accounted for fully one-fourth of total sales. A somewhat lower priority was given to institutional marketing with schools, hospitals, and similar outlets. "Economically it doesn't make sense for us to compete east of the Mississippi, (in) Chicago or Texas," Elsener commented. Tree Top would work on increasing its market share in the West and Southwest, and try to make higher profits instead of bigger sales. Transportation costs from the Pacific Northwest kept Tree Top "from trying to wedge" into distant markets. Likewise, he said, the cooperative had no big "corporate parent" to bankroll its advertising and promotional activities.[7] With the limited funds available, the management team would explore the expansion of co-packing arrangements and also probe new opportunities in the industrial ingredients marketplace, but only where profits were most likely.

On a practical note, Elsener promised the grower-members average returns over a three-year period of at least $15 per ton more than commercial market prices. Since the cooperative had seldom paid more than a $15 average above the market price, this last guarantee stood out on the list of objectives and strategies. As it turned out, the perpetual "roller-coaster" volatility of unpredictable raw product supplies and the equally mysterious pricing of foreign concentrate on the international market heavily influenced the outcome of some of these carefully conceived plans.

The mid-1990s brought a surge of expansion and reorientation at Tree Top. In September 1995, the cooperative made an agreement to acquire specified assets of California Foods in Rialto, California, which included two bottling lines and, with an option to buy, a five-year lease on an 80,000-square-foot plant and warehouse. At Rialto, the facilities were more than twice as large as the previously leased plant at City of Commerce. This calculated move indicated the importance of Los Angeles and Southern California as Tree Top's most lucrative market area. With the additional capacity at Rialto, the Selah-based firm had more opportunity to grow and increase its penetration of that nearby marketplace. Another important advantage of the Rialto plant was its co-packing arrangements with such major companies as Coca-Cola and Tropicana.[8] Under then-current plans, concentrate would be trucked from Washington to Rialto for bottling. As for the financial aspects of the deal, concluded in 1996, Tree Top paid $3.5 million to purchase the California Foods assets.

Another spurt of expansion in 1996 involved the purchase of SunRidge Foods in Sunnyside, Washington, a privately held company. After his departure from Tree Top in 1989, former CEO Dennis Colleran had been instrumental in building up SunRidge to become the third largest producer of dried apples in the United States. This acquisition gave Tree Top members an additional marketing outlet and also provided an extra supply of raw product for the ingredients business. The purchase price of SunRidge was $4.8 million. Another large expenditure in 1996 was a major warehouse addition at Selah costing $4.6 million.

Including the California Foods acquisition at $3.5 million, Tree Top had spent $12.9 million in a single year on additional facilities. As evidence of its improved financial situation since the Alar crisis, and its future prospects, there had been no difficulty getting long-term loans for most of the financing in all three deals. It was a far cry from a lending agency's advice during the Alar crisis to give up and liquidate the cooperative.

With the rise of the ingredients business, Tree Top arranged a joint venture with the PlumLife Company to manufacture and sell Just Like Shortenin', a fat-free, fruit-based substitute for shortening in baked goods. This product had the potential for an almost revolutionary effect in the baking industry. It was a substitute for fatty shortening and extended shelf-life with its moisture retention qualities for such baked goods as pizzas, bagels, breads, cookies, and mixes. In particular, the Tree Top management team expected the partnership with PlumLife to help attract those retail customers with dietary concerns.[9]

"Just Like Shortenin'."

Another marketing expansion for the ingredients division also drew on the popularity of healthy diets and featured Tree Top dried-apple products. In 1995, Randy Dusin, research scientist, and Scott Summers, manager of technical services, worked with General Mills in the development of Sweet Rewards, a line of no-fat baking mixes, including an apple cinnamon cake for snacks. Dusin and Summers helped overcome the problem of infusing the apple product with corn syrup so that the fruit would not float to the top of the batter when cooking. This process was also adopted for bagels. Because the original project involved corporate giant General Mills, the skilled collaborative work of Tree Top's research and technical staff paid off with significant profits for the cooperative and higher returns for its members.

Also in tune with dietary trends, the cooperative began furnishing fresh-cut apples for Del Monte's fruit snack cups. Likewise, in a major new retail product for healthy diets, the Selah-based firm introduced Three Apple Blend, a beverage containing only the juices of fresh-pressed apples, and no concentrate. In 2001, Tree Top marketed its own Fresh Apple Slices, using a special plastic seal that kept the fruit fresh for 21 days under refrigeration. Later, in a major promotional campaign, the cooperative hired a new business manager, Ned Rawn, whose special assignment was increasing the sales of apple slices. The fast-food chain McDonald's had already added fresh slices to its menus, and airlines and similar commercial venues also soon offered this product. [10]

A big organizational step was taken in May 1996 when Tree Top announced the restructuring of its management system. The reorganization, called "Operation Clear Focus," resulted from the development over the years of two distinctly different lines of business. Packaged goods, such as apple juice and juice-based drinks, still remained the largest division in terms of sales, but the industrial ingredients trade, such as dehydrated and low-moisture items, now accounted for one-third of sales, and was increasing rapidly. In fact, it appeared that industrial operations would almost certainly become the most profitable part of the firm in the foreseeable future. Recognizing these circumstances, the board of directors created two separate administrative lines of responsibility, each with an executive leader designated as "president." Both divisions depended on a common pipeline of raw mate-

rial, but from that point on the differences were greater than the similarities.

It was a matter of twins, but not identical twins. As CEO Frank Elsener explained it succinctly in the 1996 annual report:

The packaged goods business, which accounts for two-thirds of Tree Top's total sales, has many competitors, is regional, has shown only modest growth, is extremely price sensitive and has two and sometimes three levels in the distribution channel between Tree Top and the ultimate consumer. In contrast, the industrial segment has relatively few competitors, is international in scope, has shown strong recent growth trends, has little price sensitivity and offers an opportunity to work very closely with the customer to develop value-added products.

Elsener went on to say that both divisions were leaders in their fields, with Tree Top apple juice being the best seller in the United States, and its industrial ingredients rated first by 23 of the country's 25 food industry concerns. Board chair John E. Borton also pointed out that the separation would make it simpler to determine expenses and profits, and therefore accountability and the allocation of resources, in each case. "The reorganization treats each business as a distinct entity," Borton said, "with unique challenges and opportunities."

For president of the new Consumer Packaged Goods Division, the board named Thomas P. Stokes, who at age 46 had spent 21 years at Tree Top in various management positions. Ray Dilschneider, who was 41 years old and had been at the cooperative 17 years in a series of high-level positions, was designated as president of the Ingredient Division. They joined a slimmed-down management team, or executive committee, of only five persons, including CEO Elsener. The other team members were Lindsay Buckner, vice president of field services, and Richard Bailey, executive vice president and chief financial officer. Previously, 10 top executives had reported to the CEO, and now only 4 did so.

Lindsay Buckner.

More than ever, globalization now characterized the apple juice marketplace. Foreign concentrate made up the stock for over 50 percent of this beverage sold in the United States, which represented a 30 percent increase in only 15 years. The rising demand for juice products in far off Asia and Europe had a direct impact on the earnings of growers in Washington state. Tree Top, with its small-town Selah headquarters and a mission to serve its Pacific Northwest regional membership, had to devise a global strategy to fulfill its responsibilities. The cooperative reportedly bought concentrate on the open market only when its raw product pipeline ran short, but this practice provided little protection from international events. When the world price of concentrate soared from $5 per gallon to $12, as it did in 1992, such a dramatic change immediately affected processing costs and necessitated increased prices of Tree Top products in order to maintain the targeted level of payouts to growers.

Global marketing brought Tree Top into some unexpected, complicated situations. Coca-Cola was the corporate parent of the juice producer Minute Maid. When Coca-Cola charged in federal court that it had been deceived by six suppliers, the Federal Food and Drug Administration began an investigation of fraudulent apple concentrate with a 10 percent content of sweetener made from "chicory or Jerusalem artichoke." Like other U.S. processors, Tree Top had to publicly declare its innocence in the whole affair. And even though the cooperative announced its tenth straight year of profitability in 2002, payments to the members dropped because of large supplies of concentrate on the world market.[11]

In terms of world prominence, it is often said, the 1900s were the American century, and the 2000s are the Asian century. To some extent, Tree Top's interest in international trade at this time was most influenced by Asian countries, especially Japan and China. An unexpected drop in Japanese sales and other issues caused Tree Top to accept a restructured agreement with key partner Pokka. Under the new arrangement Pokka would continue to distribute the cooperative's products in some parts of Japan, while different brokers would sell the Tree Top brand in other local markets. The management team had held high hopes for the Japanese market, but, as already explained, the weak American dollar and other uncertainties continued to surround relations with Japanese co-packers and wholesalers.

Prolonged profits failed to materialize in that marketplace.[12] Sales in China rose slowly, and it seemed that a persistent, long-term strategy held the most promise in that communist country.

Otherwise, along with Japan and China, Tree Top had targeted Mexico for special attention. Even before the North American Free Trade Agreement (NAFTA) went into effect on January 1, 1994, sales had grown appreciably in Mexican markets, and continued to do so. Europe also opened up, first with sales in France and even a few orders from eastern Russia. In a particularly pleasing development, wholesalers in the former Soviet Union initiated contacts with International Sales Manager Eric Shetterly about selling Tree Top products in the Khabarovsk and Vladivostok parts of eastern Russia. With few supermarkets and poor drinking water, the Russians had ambitious plans to distribute juice in small retail kiosks.[13] In the early 1990s, however, total international consumer sales comprised less than 10 percent of Tree Top's total revenues, and had remained at about the same level during those years.

Although an uninviting marketplace, China took on a role of great importance in the worldwide distribution of apple concentrate. In the late 1980s, American agricultural scientists who were permitted to visit there saw little evidence that mainland China would ever present any kind of threat to the U.S. apple industry, much less challenge the supremacy of Washington state. Like its other economic and industrial accomplishments, however, China developed rapidly in apple production and moved just as swiftly toward becoming number one in that field.

Between 1995 and 1998, imports of Chinese concentrate increased by 1,200 percent. By 1999, China had surged ahead as the first-place grower and was deluging the United States with cheap concentrate. The result was a 90 percent drop in U.S. juice apple prices, with processing fruit selling at an average of $10 per ton. Some Washington growers left apples rotting on the trees rather than harvest them at a loss. In fact, many American orchardists were convinced that the Chinese had actually engaged in "dumping," and thus violated U.S. law prohibiting a foreign importer from selling goods here below production costs—in this case, reportedly 91 percent under. This practice not only resulted in a surplus of culls on the market, which depressed prices for Tree Top members, but also had an adverse effect on fresh-apple sales.[14] As previously

Pat Moss and Historical Sensitivity

Pat Moss.

As corporate communications manager for 20 years, Patricia Gail "Pat" Moss was the "voice" of Tree Top Inc. Moss grew up in Hope, Arkansas, and graduated from Harding University at Searcy with a degree emphasis in journalism. She worked as a research analyst for the Oregon State Legislative Counsel in Salem before coming to Tree Top. Hired in October 1974, at first as secretary to the president, she was later assigned to public relations. For several years, the communications duties were divided, with Moss handling internal information for the growers and employees, while John McAlister dealt with external news for the general public, government agencies, and food industry organizations. Besides regular dispatches, Moss also produced *Tree Topics*, the newsletter sent to the cooperative's members, and *Apple Corps*, the publication for employees.

When Moss was named as the first corporate communications manager, she coordinated the messages for all audiences—employees, growers, industry, community, and media. This was the role in which she had the most influence in Tree Top affairs and for which she is best remembered by retirees and long-time employees. She was not in the forefront of the Alar crisis, but did control communications in the 1990s food safety scare involving E. coli bacteria. Emphasizing the benign qualities of apple juice generally, she spent countless hours

informing the general public and the media that all Tree Top beverage products, including cider, were pasteurized, and therefore safe to drink.

Moss also became the firm's unofficial historian, although she shared that distinction for a time with retired sales manager and interim CEO Ernest L. "Ernie" Stafford, who completed a company history sometime in the 1970s.[1] As a historian, Moss began a series of interviews with past and present board members, especially those who had founded the cooperative, as well as with long-time staff personnel, while these persons were still available. As it turned out, Moss recorded and made transcripts of two sets of interviews, one in the 1980s and another 20 years later, in 2003. Along with research in company records and other sources, such as newspapers, she used these interviews to compile a unique history of Tree Top.[2]

One of Moss's main contributions was her part in publicizing Tree Top's image as a "good citizen" in the communities where its plants were located. In the same vein, she worked at opening publicity avenues with the local news media, reasoning that these localities should be aware of the firm's interest in civic uplift. At her well-attended retirement ceremony in 2005, Pat Moss was given many fond expressions of appreciation for her effective service. Looking back on her 30 years with Tree Top, she has reflected, "It was a good ride."

1. [Ernest L. Stafford], "Tree Top—The Story of Apple Juice," typewritten manuscript, Tree Top Historical files, ca. 1970s.
2. Moss typed this account on 4 X 6½ inch file cards and arranged them by categories in two metal file boxes. These boxes, the transcripts of interviews, and other material are in the Tree Top Historical Files. In the interview transcripts it is apparent that Moss knew as much about the cooperative's operations as many of the persons being interviewed.

mentioned, Tree Top representatives had declared that the cooperative bought foreign concentrate only as a last resort, to maintain production schedules.

During this period, Washington Governor Gary Locke was hard at work fulfilling his campaign pledge to use his Chinese heritage in promoting trade for the Evergreen

State with that communist country.[15] Also, the Clinton administration was engaged in highly sensitive negotiations to improve U.S.-China trade relations. Despite these ticklish circumstances, Tree Top representatives joined other Washington orchard interests in lobbying the state's congressional delegation to help initiate an investigation of

Chinese misdeeds in the international marketplace. After consultation with the U.S. Department of Commerce, the Coalition for Fair Apple Juice Concentrate Trade (FACT), administered by the industry's umbrella body, the U.S. Apple Association, filed a formal complaint against China with the International Trade Commission in June 1999. Tree Top took a pivotal role in this movement. Both Lindsay Buckner, senior vice president of field services, and Tom Hurson, vice president of finance (CPG Division), had represented the Selah-based firm with FACT and at hearings in Washington, D.C.[16]

A month later the commission announced it had found "a reasonable indication" that American business was in danger of "material injury" because of Chinese marketing practices in concentrates. A spokesperson for the Commerce Department warned, however, that a final ruling would not be made until late January 2000, well after the present year's harvest. Ironically, back when Tree Top and other processors had first declared their intention to file a complaint, the importation of Chinese concentrate had jumped by 111 percent, perhaps indicating the common belief that the final decision would go against China.

In April 2000, the Commerce Department, determining that China had engaged in dumping, imposed a duty of about 52 percent on most Chinese apple concentrates retroactive to the past August. Confirmation of this decision was expected from the International Trade Commission. Tree Top and the coalition of processors had sought a duty of 91 percent, but the cooperative's spokeswoman, Pat Moss, commented, "We feel we see the process working," adding that the tariff as imposed would provide a "deterrent" to dumping. In retrospect Washington processors as well as those in fresh-apple sales had been hit hard, and, as mentioned earlier, apples were often left on the trees to rot.[17]

It seemed that, like the Alar crisis, Tree Top had dodged another "deadly bullet" in the Chinese concentrate battle. More recently, however, the Commerce Department has used a technicality to modify its previous decision by removing many of the tariffs imposed on Chinese exporters. As a result, China still supplies concentrate for about 65 percent of America's apple juice.[18] In 2007–08, a repercussion of the concentrate controversy involved reports that some Chinese goods contained the industrial chemical melamine and other dangerous agents. Even though there

were no official warnings related to juices, Laura Prisc, Tree Top's corporate communications manager, answered a flurry of phone calls and E-mails about melamine from the media and concerned consumers.[19]

When the Tree Top cooperative was established in 1960, the market consisted almost entirely of retail grocery stores. It was a seller's paradise. Each year Tree Top produced and distributed a limited volume of products. When the manufactured goods ran out, production was shut down and the cooperative's label temporarily vanished from grocery shelves. By the 1990s, it was a buyer's market, with an expanded distribution base and many more players. Besides supermarkets, the current competitive battle for limited display space and promotional advantages involved such vendors as nursing homes, wholesale clubs, and a burgeoning array of fast-food eateries. If your product deliveries lagged, you were doomed. While planning to satisfy changing consumer demands with a wide variety of products, Tree Top also developed fresh approaches to deal with the volatile raw material supply. Under the old system a dozen packaged products was enough; now Tree Top sold 70 items with 39 flavors and blends in that category. Similar circumstances prevailed in the Industrial Ingredient Division where, in 1995 alone, eight new products were marketed, fetching an additional $750,000 in sales revenue.

In the summer of 1998, Frank Elsener announced his intention to retire as president and CEO the next spring. As his tenure neared an end, he initiated a surge of acquisitions. Anticipating bigger harvests from the new high-density tree plantings, he and the management team set out to obtain additional processing facilities and markets. First, Tree Top purchased a long-term lease on Seneca's apple sauce label, part of its apple concentrate trade, and a large processing plant at Prosser, Washington. Headquartered in New York state, Seneca manufactured apple sauce that was the first or second choice among consumers in Tree Top's core markets. Thus, the Seneca acquisition brought two obvious benefits for the cooperative's members. The growers would furnish the raw material for production of this popular apple sauce, and the Prosser plant would provide much more general processing capacity for their crops.[20]

In April 1999, Tree Top also acquired Watermill Foods of Milton-Freewater, Oregon. Since Watermill specialized in frozen fruit (cherries, apples, and plums) for the food industry, this purchase offered more processing opportuni-

ties, specifically increasing Tree Top's frozen ingredients capacity by 30 percent. In July, the Selah-based firm bought most, but not all, of the Vacu-Dry Company's dried-apple industrial ingredients line. A restructured Vacu-Dry, with headquarters at Santa Rosa, California, stayed in business, but closed its ingredients facility at Sebastopol. Those operations were shifted to Tree Top's Wenatchee facility and the Ross plant at Selah.[21] The Seneca, Watermill, and Vacu-Dry acquisitions completed an impressive sweep of expansion financed by $42 million of long-term debt. Together, the three purchases increased Tree Top's marketing potential by 50 percent.

Soon after Frank Elsener said he wanted to retire, the cooperative's board of directors authorized a national search for the next CEO. After interviewing four candidates distinguished by outstanding qualifications, the directors chose Thomas P. Stokes, then president of Tree Top's Consumer Packaged Goods Division. Born and raised on a northern Montana wheat farm, Stokes knew the cooperative's various production operations from top to bottom by firsthand experience. In fact, he had spent most of his professional life at Tree Top. Fresh out of Montana State University with a degree in industrial and management engineering, he had worked briefly as production supervi-

sor for the vegetable processing firm Lamb-Weston Inc. in Hermiston, Oregon, before joining Tree Top management at the Wenatchee plant in 1975.

As superintendent at Wenatchee, he collaborated with plant manager Kenneth Banks in rebuilding and re-equipping the facility after the fire that destroyed it. Banks had also worked at Lamb-Weston. Stokes later served as plant manager at both Wenatchee and Selah, and as vice president of operations before his two-year stint as president of packaged goods. Along the way, he had the responsibility of overseeing the cooperative's disposal of its voluminous and environmentally sensitive wastewater.

Appointed as CEO-designate in December 1998, Tom Stokes worked jointly with Frank Elsener until the following May, when Elsener formally retired. Stokes became CEO when Tree Top was enjoying the highest profits of the 1990s and consumer demand for apple juice had surged by double digits. Moreover, the acquisition of the Seneca, Watermill, and Vacu-Dry interests had been concluded during the year and the additional production and marketing potential was soon integrated into Tree Top operations. One notable source of profitability was a lucrative contract with the State of California to furnish juice for the California Women, Infants and Children (WIC) program.[22] This agreement had just been extended for another 12 months. The Industrial Ingredient Division had suffered some setbacks, but had started to recover lost ground, and the Chinese concentrate issue was under international scrutiny. In other words, the prospects for Tree Top seemed at least promising when Stokes took over as CEO.

Undercurrents of difficulty had started appearing in 1998, however, and kept on rumbling for more than three years. By the early 2000s, repeated comparisons were being made to the Alar crisis. Actually 1998 to 2004, with four straight bad years, was a longer sustained period of difficulty than the Alar episode, for the fresh-apple business and processors alike. As a Seattle newspaper described the conditions in the fall of 1998: "Throughout Washington, apple growers are reeling from a financial disaster as bad as anyone can remember. The lowest apple prices in a decade coupled with the largest crop in history, shrunken export markets and burgeoning competition overseas have some orchardists losing a lot more than their shirts." In fact, growers lost an estimated $205 million on fresh apples, and the situation with processing fruit was no better, accounting for another $33 million in losses.[23] Perhaps 20 to 30 percent, or more, of the growers in Washington state quit the apple business, some by going into bankruptcy and others by selling out, leasing, or consolidating their holdings with bigger orchards. Tree Top alone saw 300 to 400 members a year disappear from its rolls between the late 1990s and the early 2000s.

Board chair Douglas Stockwell stated in the annual report that 2001 was "one of the most challenging years in decades." Besides problems in the international marketplace, Stockwell mentioned such mundane concerns as escalating energy costs, the uncertainties of irrigation water supplies, and the limitations placed on banking lines of credit. CEO Stokes gave more details, declaring that recent events had caused a "profound structural change" in the fruit industry, including for processors like Tree Top. First, Stokes singled out the influence of globalization. For instance, Chile was attracting Tree Top customers in an

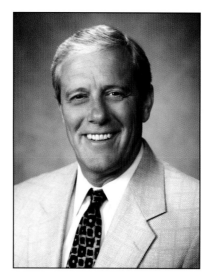

Tom Stokes.

already flattening dried-apple market. More important, huge shipments of apples and concentrate from China, as well as fresh fruit from developing nations, had almost ruined Far Eastern markets for Washington state orchardists. "World supply, dollar exchange rates and political reprisals [against the United States]," Stokes said, "now affect the… [prices] we pay growers more than a hailstorm in our region."

The second major trend transforming the fruit industry was the scale of consolidation in the marketplace. Five big corporations now controlled the retail grocery business. An immediate result was the universal demand for more "private labels," which cut into the cooperative's own sales. In this context the reputation of Tree Top as a premium product as well as consumer brand loyalty became more important than ever. Also, to remain competitive, warehouses, brokers, suppliers, and manufacturers were forced to consolidate on a comparably large scale. In dealing with all of these different groups, Tree Top had to assess the essential role of each one and determine individual strategies accordingly.

Stokes might have added yet another area of consolidation. Between 1987 and 1997, about 1,000 Washington orchardists had quit the business, leaving 10 percent of the growers controlling 62 percent of the orchard acreage in the state. The exodus claimed especially large numbers of orchardists owning 25 acres or less, while those growers holding over 500 acres more than doubled. The disastrous conditions of 1998 only increased this movement of consolidation.[24] Fewer orchardists and bigger orchards became the order of the day.

One fact became clear for the Selah-based firm. Although a pretty big fish, it was relatively small in the big pool of conglomerates and had to grow bigger or drop out of the competition. Under these circumstances, the cooperative planned to develop more sure-fire products and make acquisitions that enhanced existing operations. The purchases involving all or parts of Seneca, Watermill, and Vacu-Dry helped fulfill these goals. Likewise, the buyout of Tree Fruit Packers Inc., a Seattle processing firm

Juice Fizz, March 1996.

Tree Top Annual Report (2000).

Prosser Plant, 1999.

Tree Top juice wagon at Disneyland.

In 1994, kiosks in Vladivostok of far eastern Russia sell Tree Top products.

The Tree Top family

A contemporary view of Tree Top corporate headquarters, Selah.

Tree Top carolers, 1992.

Field Services, October 1999. Top row (l. to r.): Bill Waddoups, Dave Lewman, Brian Wheeler, Pat Moss, Ross Todorovich, Koreen Brown, Roxie Asher, Mark Burnett, Lindsay Buckner. On steps (top to bottom): Phil Giutzwiler, Chuck Running, Darla Bennett.

Tree Top CEOs of the modern era—
(l.) Frank Elsener (1992–99) and Tom
Stokes (1999–Present).

During her years at Tree Top
(1974–2005), Pat Moss was
appointed the first corporate
communications manager.
Pat Moss

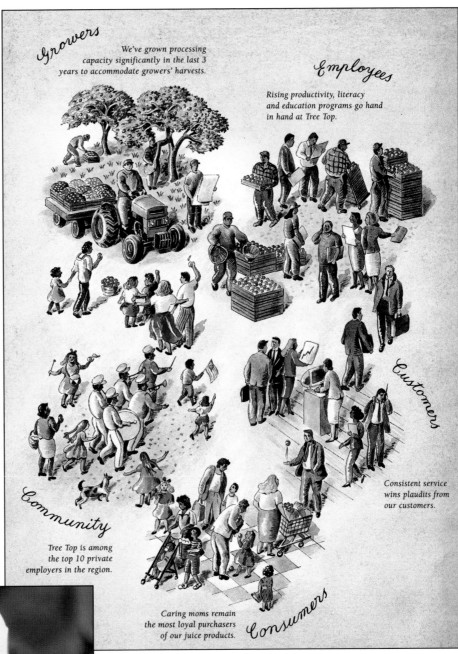

Growers

We've grown processing
capacity significantly in the last 3
years to accommodate growers' harvests.

Employees

Rising productivity, literacy
and education programs go hand
in hand at Tree Top.

Customers

Consistent service
wins plaudits from
our customers.

Community

Tree Top is among
the top 10 private
employers in the region.

Consumers

Caring moms remain
the most loyal purchasers
of our juice products.

The Tree Top vision in the early 21st century.
Tree Top Annual Report (2001).

One of the people who make
it all possible—an employee
on the production line.

Tree Top Board Members (2009)

Bruce Allen (*Southern District*).

Tom Auvil, Chairman
(*Northern District*).

Ray Colbert (*Northern District*).

Dick Cowin (*Southern District*).

Ray Keller (*Southern District*).

Ed Kershaw (*Southern District*).

Warren Morgan
(*Northern District*).

Michael Smith
(*Southern District*).

Randy Smith (*Northern District*).

Doug Stockwell
(*Northern District*).

Roger Strand (*Southern District*).

Fred Valentine
(*Northern District*).

Executive Committee

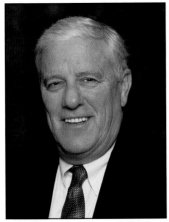

Tom Stokes (*President and Chief Executive Officer*).

Nancy Buck (*Vice President Legal Services*).

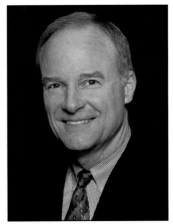

Lindsay Buckner (*Sr. Vice President Field Services*).

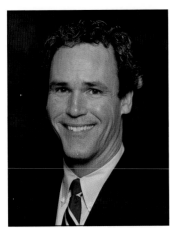

Dan Hagerty (*Sr. Vice President Sales & Marketing CPG*).

Tom Hurson (*Sr. Vice President Ingredient & Foodservice Sales and President NW Naturals*).

Dwaine Brown (*Vice President Finance and Chief Financial Officer*).

Gary Price (*Vice President Operations*).

Scott Washburn (*Vice President Human Resources*).

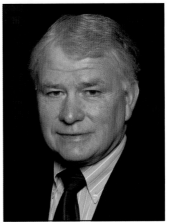

Gerald Kobes (*Vice President Engineering and Technical Support— retired Aug. 2009*).

Tree Top Apple Juice
Cure for Homesickness

Recent studies claim that children who drink lots of apple juice may be less likely to develop asthma and may have healthy brains, and juice also could ward off heart disease and cancer. None of this research mentions a cure for homesickness, but one woman's experience does present strong unscientific evidence to that effect. Nancy Hall grew up in eastern Washington at Pullman before leaving to attend Western Washington University, Bellingham, where she married a fellow student. Later, she and her husband returned to Pullman, where he received a master's degree in city management before they moved 1,700 miles away to Kansas City. As a new mother in a strange city, and far from familiar surroundings for the first time, Nancy was homesick for the Pacific Northwest. While shopping at the supermarket one day, a distinctive and familiar label caught her eye and reminded her of home. She immediately bought a gallon bottle of Tree Top apple juice.

The Hall kids; (l. to r.) Zach, Kelsey, and Erin.
Nancy Hall

As Nancy tells the story, she and her husband started drinking toasts of apple juice to the rugged volcanic peaks, majestic waterways, and rolling wheat fields they had left behind, and it helped ease the pain of being away. These toasts became a regular family ritual. And, when their son was old enough to drink from a cup, she frequently gave him apple juice as part of a balanced diet. The young boy soon developed such a discerning taste for Tree Top, Hall says, that he would stubbornly shake his head and turn his mouth away from other brands, a preference he has continued for his 24 years. In time, the family moved back to the Northwest at Olympia, with two more children added to the fold. According to Nancy, the newest members of the family had also started drinking Tree Top apple juice at an early age and had long since adopted their older brother's exclusive taste. In fact, as independent-minded teenagers, they characteristically declared that other brands tasted, well, "Weird!"

As with any company's retail product, brand loyalty is always welcomed and encouraged. Probably few other grocery items, based on Nancy Hall's convincing experience, can boast that they have helped soothe the agonizing pangs of homesickness. Moreover, besides calming homesickness in adults, Tree Top apple juice apparently can become a life-long preference for those who start consuming it at a young age.[1]

---

1. In the 1997 annual report, Lisa Rice, mother of a young son, Danny, told a similar story about a generational preference for Tree Top apple juice. "I grew up with Tree Top," Rice commented," and now my son, Danny, is growing up with it too."

specializing in frozen cherries, became a significant step in that direction. In particular, Tree Fruit, whose operations were transferred to the Milton-Freewater facility, had an impressive list of regular customers, a welcome addition to Tree Top's marketing clout. "[Such] acquisitions also strengthened our non-member business [not under contract]," CEO Stokes said, "which includes frozen cherries and a variety of specialty fruit concentrates." In a competitive context, "bulking up" with acquisitions also gave Tree Top more leverage in dealing with the consolidation it faced on every front.[25]

In a nutshell, because of both domestic and international influences, the Selah cooperative and its membership faced "a constellation of unknowns" and a "minefield" of uncertainty. Stokes explained the complex situation to the growers in down-to-earth terms:

You wrestle with pivotal questions like what varieties to plant and how much to invest as you seek a stable future and positive bottom line in today's uncertain business climate. Your Cooperative has similar questions…Consumers are getting tougher to read, their needs more fragmented, their options—particularly when it comes to food and drink—almost limitless. The cost of introducing new products is escalating. Our customers have enormous negotiating power.

Nancy Buck joined Tree Top in 1984, and today serves as Vice President for Legal Services.

And the immediate results were obvious. Beginning in 2001, the Washington state fruit industry redefined and reoriented itself, especially as a player in the world market. And the old business "model" used by Tree Top and its grower-members underwent a full-scale overhaul as well. At the insistence of Bill Charbonneau, the Tree Top cooperative had been incorporated as a private corporation. In the future the Selah firm would operate more on the principles of a corporation. Since 20 percent of the members supplied 80 percent of the raw product, those growers, some of whom had accrued equities (invested ownership) of $2 or $3 million in the cooperative, would become something like stockholders.[26]

For the 2002–03 crop year, Tree Top recorded net proceeds of $30.1 million, or $2.3 million more than the year before, which was the highest income per ton in the past five years on the lowest processing tonnage. Yet some complications accompanied this impressive report. Mother Nature had been unkind, as *Tree Topics* described this

perennial challenge to orchardists: "Cool spring weather initially affected the potential for a large crop, capped off by a late-October freeze that further damaged the late-maturing varieties not yet harvested." In addition, according to a Seattle business publication, Tree Top's "return on juice sales was squeezed between tough competition from apple juice concentrate from China and reduced availability of juice apples from Washington growers due to a smaller-than-usual crop."[27] With the smallest volume of raw material since 1988, the cooperative processed 390,000 tons, down over 20 percent from 492,000 tons the previous year. At the same time the limited availability of fruit increased the supply-and-demand price paid to growers by 67 percent, or $127 per ton for peelers; 43 percent, or $67 for juice fruit; and 40 percent, or $29 for pears.

The increased prices to growers and the maintenance of full-service operations for a low volume of raw product cut into profit margins. Moreover, since sales of the old reliable apple beverage had declined, the cooperative initiated a counter measure to take up the slack in profits by trying out alternate products made from the same juice. The most notable of these ventures was a new snack food called Flat Fruit that came in three varieties of fruit bars.[28] Manufactured from Pacific Northwest apple concentrate and pear purees by the Canadian associate firm Sun-Rype Products, the new line was aimed at the youthful and healthy diet crowds. Flat Fruit remained in the familiar lineup of Tree Top offerings for about five years but failed to "catch on" and was discontinued. Actually the fate of these tasty fruit bars probably told less about their quality than about Tree Top's perennial problem of a limited promotional and advertising budget. Sizable amounts were required to introduce and keep consumer attention focused on new products like Flat Fruit. In turn, such increased expenditures could result in minimal support for the cooperative's established retail lineup—for example, in the ever-lasting struggle for shelf space in supermarkets. Again, the subsidiaries of giant private conglomerates could tap the deep pockets of their corporate parents for virtually unlimited advertising funds, but Tree Top did not have that advantage.

Difficulties continued to arise in fiscal 2004. Not only was processing tonnage the smallest in eight years, but also three consecutive short harvests had tested the reoriented Tree Top to the limit. Newly acquired production facilities operated at reduced capacity. Other plants stood idle or worked on curtailed schedules while waiting for raw material. In fact, management promptly shut down processing at Selah and cut back on production at the Prosser and Milton-Freewater plants.

Faced with these conditions, and after "much anguished debate," it was decided to buy foreign concentrate for use in retail juice items. These purchases were "rigorously tested" in Tree Top laboratories, it was carefully explained, and the cooperative's own technical staff members had inspected and certified the original production facilities. In fact, Tree Top representatives had performed inspections even in isolated ports of China. Anticipating renewed grower opposition to the purchase of concentrate, the management team emphasized that a current drive to increase membership rolls would undoubtedly help alleviate future shortages of raw product.

Regardless of rank-and-file sentiment, it was absolutely necessary to buy foreign concentrate—or lose long-term contracted markets—when Pacific Northwest raw product supplies fell short. Even with the purchase of concentrate, the marketing staff scrambled to fill promised orders. On the bright side in 2004, total income of $29.4 million remained about the same as the year before, despite a drop in processing tonnage from 392,000 to 337,000, or a 14-percent decrease. By using "resourcefulness, ingenuity, and plenty of elbow grease," Tree Top miraculously managed to pay an average of $95 per ton to growers, or a 10 percent increase.

Predictions of a big crop year ahead and the dedication to growth led to the purchase of Northwest Naturals of Bothell, Washington, which produced wholesale fruit sweeteners and various forms of concentrates for beverages, ice cream, and the like. Now a wholly owned subsidiary of Tree Top, Northwest Naturals has the distinctive capacity of supplying organic specialties. To provide more good news, sales of the cooperative's fresh-apple slices had grown appreciably and showed promise for the future. "Watch for a steady stream of new products," the 2004 annual report confidently advised.

The board of directors saw that changing conditions of the early 2000s required further honing of the evolving business model. As usual, the problem of a reliable raw material pipeline had reared its head again. First and foremost, management somehow had to harmonize the raw material available, and future supplies, with demands of the market. In addition, the cooperative needed a different system of measuring much-discussed "profitability." The present system, which gauged profits on the basis of returns and earnings per ton of fruit delivered, might work in the short-term, but was of little help for long-term planning. Lastly, the challenges of the 21st century necessitated a reorganization of the management structure. Implementation of this objective might determine the success of the other initiatives.

Eight years earlier, in 1996, it had been logical to separate Consumer Packaged Goods and Industrial Ingredient into two distinct business lines with a president over each. Since then, the acquisition of several firms with various operations and the development facilities that could turn out multiple products tended to erase the divisional distinctions. As a result, Consumer Packaged Goods and Industrial Ingredient were returned to their previous positions in the corporate structure and headed by a vice president. Besides Tom Stokes as president and CEO, the new top management, and executive committee, had nine vice presidents in charge of operations, marketing, human resources, finances, and so on. A task force started a thoroughgoing assessment of all Tree Top operations, with the assignment of devising a long-term plan that specified goals and how to obtain them. By necessity, however, Tree Top would operate on continually evolving strategies in the tempestuous times ahead, no matter what basic blueprint was submitted. 🍎

Endnotes

1. Of the four departed executives, Robert M. Dennis, vice president of field services, had retired because of health difficulties.
2. "Troubled Tree Top Names Interim CEO," *Seattle Times*, June 15, 1989, H1.
3. For the essential facts in this case, see *Auvil v. CBS "60 Minutes"* 800 F. Supp. 928 (E.D. Wash. 06/5/1992), and two articles online: *New York Times*, November 29, 1990, and Timothy Egan, "Apple Growers Bruised and Bitter after Alar Scare," *New York Times*, July 9, 1991.
4. On news of Tree Top's continuing recovery from the Alar crisis, see "Apple Industry Says Concerns Are Political," *Seattle Times*,

January 22, 1990; *Seattle Times*, June 9, 1990, July 1, 1991, November 26, 1991—all online. In the *Puget Sound Business Journal*, July 2, 1990, online, John McAlister, Tree Top public relations spokesperson, summed up the Alar episode and reported that the cooperative, although now leaner after the "panic," had regrouped, and that its earnings were up following the easing of public concern about the health effects caused by the chemical spray.

5. *Apple Corps*, special edition, July 1992.
6. In 1994, the Tree Top board eliminated the Season Average Option, leaving in place only the Current Market Option.
7. Bill Virgin, "Tree Top Presses Ahead with Expansion Plans Despite Overabundance of Apples, Competitors Bearing Fruit," *Seattle Post-Intelligencer*, October 2, 1995, B3; *Wenatchee World*, October 14, 1993, online.
8. *Apple Corps*, November/December 1995.
9. *Apple Corps*, September/October 1995, January/February 1996, April 1998.
10. *Apple Corps*, November/December 1995, June 1997, February 1998, May 2001, March 2004.
11. "Adulterated Apple Juice Prompts a Federal Probe," *Seattle Post-Intelligencer*, February 27, 1996, B6; *Seattle Times*, October 14, 2002.
12. Reportedly some Japanese firms had the reputation of at first working with foreign concerns and then absorbing them. A more explicit example of such tenuous relations involved the U.S. fresh-apple trade. Japan had imposed selective scientific testing standards to block almost all U.S. fresh-apple imports for some 20 years. In June 2005, the World Trade Organization issued a decision discrediting those standards and favoring the United States in the dispute. U.S. fresh-apple marketers had lost an estimated $143.4 million because of Japan's restrictions. Press release, Office of the U.S. Trade Representative, June 23, 2005, online.
13. *Apple Corps*, January/February 1995.
14. Michael Paulson, "Apple Growers Accuse Beijing of 'Dumping': China Blamed for Low U.S. Prices: Producers Lobby for

Punishment," *Seattle Post-Intelligencer*, September 20, 1999, A1. Actually, as early as 1994 or 1995 China had bypassed the United States in apple production, and by 1999 grew an estimated seven times more than American orchards. See also, Editorial, "Diverse Group Supports Juice Concentrate Tariff," *Yakima Herald-Tribune*, September 17, 1999.
15. *Yakima Herald-Tribune*, October 24, 1996, B8.
16. *Apple Corps*, January 2000.
17. Associated Press dispatch, in *Seattle Times*, April 8, 2000, online.
18. U.S. Apple Association, news release, November 19, 2002. All online: *Seattle Times*, September 4, 2005; *New York Times*, July 1, 2007; *Dallas Morning News*, December 8, 2007. See Sung-Yeol Cho, "An Economic Analysis of the Washington Apple Industry," Ph.D. dissertation, Washington State University, 15–23, for a brief scholarly commentary on China's influence on the Washington apple industry.
19. *Dallas Morning News*, December 8, 2007, online.
20. It should be noted that Tree Top purchased only certain parts of Seneca's operations, including the right to use its trademark apple sauce label, but did not buy the entire New York state firm.
21. "Tree Top Buys Vacu-dry's Ingredient Business," *Puget Sound Business Journal*, June 24, 1999, online.
22. Under the next contract, Tree Top had to share the WIC business with other vendors.
23. *Seattle Times*, October 3, 1999, online.
24. Ibid.
25. *Yakima Valley Business Times*, May 11, 2001, B-5.
26. One of the advantages of joint incorporation was that cooperatives could collaborate among themselves on such matters as prices, which would be unlawful as collusion for private corporations.
27. Quotes are from *Tree Topics*, February 2003, and *Puget Sound Business Journal*, November 10, 2003, online.
28. Flat Fruit had a companion product in Fruit & Energy bars, which, in turn, had a vegetable variety.

Tree Top Values

Integrity—We do the right thing, communicating openly and honestly, exhibiting behaviors consistent with our words, and are accountable for our results.

Respect for Others—We build strong relationships—with growers, employees, customers, and business partners—based on mutual respect and support, valuing each other's experience, opinions, and diversity.

Corporate Citizenship—We are conscientious about our impact on the environment and in our communities, and do what we can to make a positive difference.

Leadership at Every Level—We adapt to our dynamic business environment, address challenges strategically, strive to improve performance and processes, and lead by example.

Simplicity and Practicality—We strive for clear, concise communication abiding by few and simple policies, using simple solutions to avoid bureaucracy and complexity.

Tree Top 2009 Annual Report.

Chapter 6

The First 50 Years in Perspective

For Tree Top to close a functioning plant for good was like cutting off an arm, particularly if it involved a facility that went all the way back to the Charbonneau era of private ownership. In the late 1950s, after frustration with Wenatchee zoning regulations, Charbonneau in his typical style had told off local officials and constructed his new plant for the production of apple concentrate at Cashmere. The Tree Top cooperative later bought an already established processing installation at nearby Wenatchee. Since then, both plants had remained key elements in the Tree Top holdings. That is, until 2008, when the board of directors, upon the recommendation of the management team, ordered closure of the Cashmere plant.

It is tempting to say that the demise of this venerable facility came in a straight line because the price of Chinese concentrate in West Coast markets prevented the cooperative from providing a reasonable return on concentrate produced at Cashmere. In other words, with the overall equation of "profitability" and financial returns to the grower-members always uppermost in mind, it made no sense to compete in that market by continuing concentrate operations at Cashmere, which was all that the plant did. Indeed, this was one of the reasons for the closure, but the story is more involved than that.

Cashmere plant, January 2001.

Closing the Cashmere facility also resulted from Tree Top's continually adjusting business model of the 2000s, which called for quick assessments, immediate decisions, and deep changes when necessary. In this case, flexibility as well as profitability were at stake, most notably by the savings in operational expenses through the closure. Significantly, more apples had formerly been grown in the

Northern District, but now the Yakima district to the south probably produced one-third more than the Wenatchee vicinity and the Okanogan country. Because of this, in addition to the fact the industry overall was growing fewer processor apples, Cashmere's concentrate production could be shifted to Prosser, where more diversified processing existed.[1] Although a difficult decision, it made good sense from a business standpoint.

Quick decision making had become the order of the day since the Alar crisis, followed by the economic shock wave of 1998–2002. The Cashmere closure was not the first such shut-down, although it did have the distinction of being the first member of the starting lineup sent to the locker room. In another case, the plant at Milton-Freewater, Oregon, which processed frozen fruit, had been purchased from Watermill Foods in 1999 and fully integrated into the Tree Top system. But the long-term plan for the 2000s submitted by a special task force confronted the management team with some challenging choices.

As one of these determined decisions, the CEO had announced that the Milton-Freewater plant would be closed in December 2005, and its production lines shifted to other facilities. The distance from other Tree Top installations, savings in transportation expenses, extra capacity elsewhere, and general efficiency concerns were among the reasons given for the action. Reportedly, prospective buyers were ready to purchase the property. It might seem inconsistent that about the same time the Milton-Freewater unit was shuttered, Tree Top built a new, thoroughly up-to-date facility at Selah to turn out fresh apple slices, currently a hot-selling item. But this was the kind of flexibility the new business landscape required.

Implementation of the long-term plan, CEO Stokes said, would soon bring other changes to make the various production units more efficient and profitable.

Likewise, the plan envisioned large-scale growth in a new direction. In October 2008, the cooperative purchased a thriving processing firm, the Sabroso Company, whose main product was fruit puree. With 180 workers and annual sales of $90 million, Sabroso had plants in Medford and Woodburn, Oregon, as well as Oxnard, California. Besides puree, it also produced ingredients from apples, pears, peaches, apricots, and berries for use in baby food, bakery items, various drinks, and ice cream.[2] The mere size of this new acquisition, in addition to its scope of operations, set the pace for Tree Top in the 21st century.

As if the challenges of globalization were not enough, the domestic economic situation also played a part in the evolution of Tree Top's manufacturing and marketing strategies. The first priority for management, of course, was to maintain balance between the available raw product and retail shelf-space commitments, as well as industrial ingredients contracts. But domestic economic conditions had a direct bearing on decision-making. Not surprisingly, Tree Top's economic difficulty during the Alar episode, when a major bank lender threatened to pinch off credit, had been exacerbated by the national recession of 1990–91. Likewise, the global alarm that sounded for the apple industry in 1998–2001 was accompanied by the so-called "Dot-Com Recession" of that period. Now, as the first decade of the 2000s draws to a close and Tree Top's 50th anniversary approaches, the United States is experiencing the worst economic recession since the Great Depression of the 1930s. Inevitably, the Tree Top board of directors and the management team had to consider these circumstances, as well as the uncertainties ahead, in closing the Cashmere plant and whatever future actions might be necessary to tighten and fine-tune the cooperative's overall system. In this vein, the Tree Top leadership decided, in 2009, to close the bottling plant at Rialto, California. Cutbacks in federal funding for nutritional programs that provided juice for low-income mothers and infants, as well as other factors, limited the usefulness of this facility. The business model of the 2000s called for the Selah-based cooperative to be big, alert, and tough-minded.

Tree Top had special strengths, however, that helped it survive economic hard times better than some other concerns in the food industry. Apple juice had become associ-ated with a proper diet. Moreover, with an estimated 90 percent of that beverage consumed by kids five years old and under, it was unlikely that parents, even in a recession, would deprive their children of a food product considered basic to good health. In the same vein, the cooperative's ingredients division manufactured several items that went into such products as breakfast cereal, which always had a prominent place on the shelves of most every household pantry. At first glance, this advantage might seem unimportant, but the economic impact of ingredients sold in thousands of tons made a big difference in the budget. For the apple industry generally, including Tree Top as a processor, one of the latest dietary appeals has emphasized that apples help fight the common problem of childhood obesity. One research specialist in the field, while extolling the virtues of this fruit, has commented that apple products are "competing for stomach space with taco chips," when offering a tempting alternative to kids.[3]

For the Tree Top board and management—constantly watching the raw product pipeline, the global market, and home-front economic trends—it was also essential to keep the basics in mind. The primary concern of the cooperative's members has always been their stake in the fresh-fruit market and the effect that hailstorms, freezing weather, and insect and parasite infestations might have on those prices. Processing generally was considered rather secondary to them. Yet when the growers' harvests went to the warehouse for handling, usually about 25 percent of their apple crops were separated as culls, or sortouts, and sent to processing plants. Traditionally, of this 25 percent, Tree Top usually took 15 percent or more. So far, it was all simple arithmetic, but there were challenges.

In the industry crisis of the early 2000s, the total acreage of apples grown in Washington state had dropped from about 200,000 to 175,000. When replanting occurred in a few years, the common practice was to put in 800, or even more, trees per acre instead of the previous 300. In the Columbia Basin, for example, an acreage that shortly before had been an alfalfa field could become a producing orchard in three years with 900 "precocious" semi-dwarf trees per acre of the Fuji variety.[4] The new tree varieties and the improved care given them by the orchardists often reduced the number of culls to perhaps 15 to 18 percent of the harvest. Tree Top's share was reduced accordingly, which created another potential shortage for the cooperative's management to consider. With so many young trees, and especially of new varieties, it now was doubly difficult to make accurate predictions of crop yields. However, the huge increase in overall apple production partially ameliorated this situation. There were fewer growers, but bigger orchards. Previously, some members might deliver an average of 50 tons a year, while now some sent 30,000 tons a year.

On the other hand, strange things could happen. The 2008 record Washington apple crop promised high profits until it was discovered that the harvest would produce an unusually large proportion of small fruit, one-third of the total yield instead of one-fourth or less. Not only did the young trees and different varieties make predictions of crop yields difficult, but there was no reliable method of foreseeing an unusual number of small apples. Much of the fruit this size customarily went to processors like Tree Top, but now many orchardists shopped around for the best price in a cash market that had plummeted to about $20 per ton.[5] Tree Top managed to acquire an adequate supply of raw product despite the turmoil affecting the pipeline's flow. Under similar circumstances, a board chair had wisely observed that every year seemed to be "uniquely difficult" in the processing business. All of these changes and uncertainties made the job especially problematical for the field representatives, who had the responsibility of gathering information contributing to the predictions of yearly harvests.

Ray Keller—board member (1987–Present) and chairman (1998–2000).

The cooperative's mission of diversification and finding additional markets for the growers' crops has meant that the research and development component has been kept busy coming up with a steady stream of new products. At the same time, the marketing staff has had the dual responsibility of encouraging more sales of basic items, such as juice, blends, and apple sauce, as well as promoting the new offerings. Over the past 50 years, Tree Top has been notably successful in creating new products and opening more marketing opportunities. Starting with apple juice, the product list has grown to a variety of blends, from standard apple sauce to several flavors, from dried apples to an array of ingredients for the industrial food industry, and from dried fruit snacks to packaged fresh apple slices. Sales of apple juice and cider

have slipped, but remain the backbone of the retail trade, with blends and apple sauce bolstering this market. Recent novelty items such as apple fries, featured at the Burger King fast food chain, and "trim," a juice drink for weight-conscious consumers,[6] as well as Flat Fruit, the packaged snack food bar in three varieties, have been introduced with an eye on marketing trends. Despite a restricted supply of fruit raised by organic standards, Tree Top has filled as many of these orders as it could. During the early 2000s, the cooperative also became, whenever its resources permitted, the main U.S. vendor for apple concentrate.

In 2006, to match the changing times, Tree Top developed a brand new logo and tagline, or slogan. A large "TREE TOP," and underneath it in smaller letters, "Real Fruit from Real People," were inscribed on a background of luxuriant green tree leaves. Signifying that the cooperative now processed a wide variety of fruit, the familiar red apple was shifted from the front to the back label. By 2010, the most notable change in marketing, however, had appeared in sales statistics showing that industrial ingredients were impressively more profitable than retail consumer goods.

As the 50th anniversary year of 2010 approached, the key words "transition," "reposition," "restructuring," and "adaptive" often appeared in the firm's corporate documents. And the management team tended to equate "down-sizing" with "right-sizing." Not surprisingly, these terms often referred, either directly or indirectly, to the fluctuating supply of raw product. In 2008, CEO Tom Stokes declared that, based on recent trends, "the years of abundant processor apples are over." One of the main reasons, as he had pointed out earlier, was that apples previously destined for processing now were sold on the fresh-fruit market. Other trends were also at work, such as increased handling fees charged by the warehouses, which tended to limit the number of lower value culls being delivered. In fact, many growers let this kind of fruit drop to the ground from the tree limbs because there was so little profit in harvesting it.

Stokes implied that Tree Top management could no longer state that an endless annual surplus of fruit lay ahead and the fluctuating supply pipeline was a problem of the past. Henceforth Tree Top would have "to do more with less." The watchword of the future would be "value." This meant focusing on value added above the price growers could get elsewhere, not on the volume, or tonnages, delivered. In turn, it meant production of the most profitable items and cutting back on those with the least payoffs, or those of marginal added value.

From now on, board chair Bruce Allen added, Tree Top would not apply its limited resources to maintaining all the facilities that were necessary to receive bumper crops, whether they came in or not. In short, the cooperative had changed its policy of "take it all" to one to "maximize returns." Accordingly, the management team was authorized "to redefine the relationships" with growers by modifying the membership contracts so that future tonnages delivered were based strictly on individual market rights, with no leeway allowed. In the past, if members had 50 market rights, they could bring in all of their cull fruit, no matter how large the tonnage. Under the modified agreements, 50 market rights would entitle the grower to deliver no more than 50 tons. On the other hand, probably the most notable departure from previous policies was the emphasis on member loyalty to the cooperative—and the binding commitment to send, without fail, 50 tons to Tree Top in normal crop years.[7] In short, tonnages would be predictable, and capped, at a level that matched the sales base.

CEO Stokes and his management team, with strong backing from the Tree Top board, had launched a change in tactics. Instead of spending time trying to estimate the fluctuating supply pipeline, they would devote their efforts to stabilization by establishing a predetermined, steady level of the cooperative's operations, knowing pretty well beforehand what they could expect through membership deliveries.[8] If an additional supply was needed, it could be purchased on the cash market, but the Tree Top board became committed to not using foreign concentrate. This pledge against imports made possible the inauguration of a distinctive new advertising campaign; updated labels stated that the product contained 100 percent USA-grown fruit.[9]

After nearly 50 years, the cooperative had devised an equity system that solved the erratic flow of raw product. Tree Top had become a full-service processor, but for its membership only, and under clearly specified terms. In the process of making new contracts, the cooperative verified

that it had 1,062 members. Over the years, the number of members contracted with the cooperative had decreased, but the total amount of acreage involved increased significantly. This profile of fewer growers, but larger holdings, reflected a continuing trend in the overall Washington apple industry. Under the new contracts, members were required to deliver a specified amount of fruit for processing every year. Because of the new requirements, and the fluctuation of natural attrition, the membership has dropped from earlier years.

Tree Top has always been known as a national and international leader in the processing industry. Nowhere was this recognition more obvious than in the evolution of machinery and equipment. The fundamental process of four phases has stayed about the same—that is, extraction of the fruit followed by treatment, filtering, and then bottling or, in time, further processing into apple sauce, ingredients, or "essence" for concentrate. Frequent modernization of the mechanized system has been a top priority. For instance, the early approach employed for ingredients relied on natural gas flames to dry batches of fruit; then, a shift was made to "continuous drying," instead of periodic batches. Although old-fashioned sorting by hand has continued along the fruit-laden conveyor belts, modern-day video cameras, laser-like sensors, and other new technological devices have taken over most of the peeling-to-core examination for quality. Jets of compressed air have proved effective in tossing out rejects.

Bill Charbonneau's introduction of frozen apple concentrate in Washington, and developing the required production equipment, ranks as one of the greatest technological and marketing achievements in the cooperative's 50-year history. By comparison, for the overall apple industry, controlled atmosphere storage, known as CA, has comparable importance. In this system, apples are almost literally made dormant in large, sealed storage structures with oxygen levels reduced to 1 or 2 percent, usually by the introduction of nitrogen gas. Temperature, humidity, oxygen, and carbon dioxide readings are carefully monitored. The fruit is "awakened" months later, ripened, and shipped to market. Tree Top benefits from CA because much of its raw product supply comes from warehouses with culls and fresh apples stored together in those facilities. Old-style refrigeration, which is still used by warehouses for some fruit, provides storage for three or four months, whereas controlled

Mechanical Updates

The lowly but effective apple bin has long been a symbol of the fruit business. By the 1980s, however, reliance on these large wooden containers was being challenged by various new methods of "bulk dumping." A mechanized ramp could now simply elevate a "bulk-hopper" truck at an angle, allowing the dumping of an entire load of fruit out the back of a semi-trailer. Or, trucks themselves might have hydraulic lifts to raise the trailers and dump a cargo out the back. In other cases, specially equipped heavy-duty trucks at a plant could hitch up to semi-trailers for this task. Other bulk trailers could release their loads through doors in the bottom, while others had hydraulic equipment that unloaded fruit by tilting containers sideways. Generally, only juice apples are handled in bulk dumping; peeler fruit would be bruised by this form of transportation.

Bulk receiving at the Selah plant.

Perhaps the most interesting automated devices to watch in action have been the successors of an early mobile robot nicknamed "Matilda," which stacked with precision boxes of dried and dehydrated products.[1] The introduction of labor-saving mechanical and automated devices has resulted in a significant reduction of manual labor. On the other hand, modern equipment has required the hiring of highly-trained staff with special technical skills. Of even more importance, Tree Top's use of bulk-hopper trucking has saved the warehouses significant costs previously spent in handling traditional wooden containers. Bins are still used, but in fewer numbers. This contribution is one more way that Tree Top has helped provide a financial "floor" under the overall apple industry.[2]

1. *Apple Corps*, May 2000, shows "Matilda" in action at the Ross plant in Selah. The name was chosen by the plant employees.
2. *Yakima Valley Business Times*, May 11, 2001, B-5. Customarily, warehouses have owned most of the bins. Since they now operate some of the bulk-hopper trucking, these warehouses also benefit financially from the fees charged for this service.

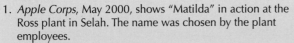
Ross plant's robotic palletizer, "Matilda."

atmosphere storage allows year-round deliveries. For Tree Top, this regulation of the raw product flow has helped stabilize production and marketing.[10]

Introduced in Washington in 1957, CA has gained attention as a "glamorous" scientific achievement. On the other hand, Charbonneau's pioneering role with frozen apple concentrate is usually regarded, if at all, as rather unremarkable.[11] Yet Charbonneau's notable contribution, made with the consultation of government researchers and private manufacturers, was a significant breakthrough that essentially changed the production and marketing landscape of the fruit processing business. For shipments from the far-corner Pacific Northwest, the reduction in apple juice volume by a significant compression ratio has paid off handsomely in lower transportation costs.

Often, Tree Top staff members who knew what was needed in the workplace have drawn up the designs for innovative equipment, while specialized manufacturers have done the rest by contract. In this pioneering role, the Selah-based cooperative has advanced the overall industry. Other processors have quickly adopted or purchased these innovations. Perhaps a more common practice has been for skilled employees to continue making incremental improvements in the machinery on hand, with these modifications resulting in better efficiencies than what the original design promised to deliver.

Recently, in the spirit of globalization, the Washington fruit industry has often turned to foreign countries for innovations—such as Belgium and New Zealand for packing equipment, Canada for instruments to monitor storage facilities, and Japan for tractors, not to mention Europe for tree root stocks, and Japan and New Zealand for different apple varieties. As for processing itself, Tree Top might install a piece of plant equipment made in Germany, Italy, or Poland, but overall has probably made relatively fewer foreign purchases.

Tree Top regarded the updating and improvement of mechanical systems as an integral part of its mission in developing more outlets for the grower-owners' crops. For the first few years, apple juice processing simply involved pressing the fruit against a screen, and then pumping the pulp through filters composed of porous rock-like material. Seeking more efficiency in separating the liquid portions, management obtained considerably better results by installing a centrifuge-operational process. Later, the older

filter structure was replaced with membrane cartridges that could be reused after cleaning. Another advancement came in a chemical treatment with enzymes in large decanters. Early in the electronic information era, Tree Top began using computers to estimate the flow of raw product, monitor every phase of production, record the status of inventories, communicate with brokers, and keep track of financial matters. Obviously, a main objective in most of these technological changes was efficiency. For instance, the shift in the filtration process from porous screens to a centrifuge basis cut the time of this production phase from 14 hours to only 4.

Charbonneau's production schedule had depended on the seasonal availability of different apple varieties. In the fall, he sold juice blended from Red Delicious and Jonathan varieties, and in the early spring, Delicious, Romes, and/or Winesaps. As late as the mid-1990s, Red Delicious made up 75 percent of all the apples processed by Tree Top. At the time, Red Delicious was prevalent in Washington orchards. Golden Delicious had been a favorite, but other varieties quickly caught up or moved ahead, especially Gala and Fuji. Granny Smith apples, first introduced in the United States in 1972 by the legendary orchardist Grady Auvil, had soon become a strong market contender in Washington, but by the mid-1990s had fallen behind a combination composed of such varieties as Jonagold and Braeburn. Due to the large supply and poor returns, some growers virtually abandoned Red Delicious, turning to those varieties with such exotic names as Ambrosia, Pacific Rose, Pink Lady, and Honeycrisp. In short, driven by the fresh-apple market, the number of varieties increased dramatically and the cooperative received fewer tonnages of Red Delicious. That variety now makes up about 35 percent of the apples delivered to Tree Top. [12]

In Tree Top's current processing operations, the mainstays as peelers for ingredients are such varieties as Golden Delicious, Fuji, and Granny Smith. Tree Top apple juice was traditionally made from a mix of Romes and Golden Delicious. In 1997, the cooperative initiated its "most ambitious product launch in years"[13] with the introduction of Three Apple Blend, containing fresh-pressed juices from Red Delicious, Golden Delicious, and Granny Smith. Extensive market analysis was involved in the development of this new beverage. It was a well-known fact that children five or under consumed about 90 percent of the apple juice sold. Since adults tended to be more discriminating, the challenge was to produce a fruit drink that would satisfy a more sophisticated standard. Also, because taste tests showed that many adult volunteers could distinguish between fresh juice and concentrate, the Three Apple Blend was manufactured from only the freshest fruit.[14] At about the same time, the cooperative marketed Tree Top Grower's Best, a beverage requiring refrigeration and sold in large 64-ounce bottles and 8-ounce six-packs. The strategy with these sizes was aimed at getting this Tree Top product on the family refrigerator shelves alongside orange juice. As the 21st century approached, Tree Top also began catering to consumer demand involving exotic fruit, such as mangoes, tangerines, and blueberries, by introducing beverages containing some of those flavors. The Prosser plant could concentrate virtually any type of fruit, which allowed Tree Top to keep up with ever-changing popular tastes.[15]

Tree Top's two major business divisions, consumer goods and industrial ingredients, gave rise to a prioritization of the different fruit received. After a lengthy study, the board of directors in early 1983 placed a premium and a higher price on peelers used in industrial ingredients, than for juicers, used mainly for juices. Actually, the new system simply recognized the growing importance of the industrial ingredients trade and the different processing fruit involved. It was a matter of formally endorsing the facts of life. For instance, Sunkist, Post, and Betty Crocker were buying several thousand tons of custom-made, dried or frozen items for their product lines, such as fruit rolls, cookies, cereal, and cake mixes. Realistically, Tree Top operates with a single "pool" sytem with various categories given a priority for delivery and differential value when needed in the production cycle. Nevertheless, peelers still bring a higher price.

Innovative packaging materials also gave Tree Top an opportunity to set an example in the field. Until the early 1980s, the cooperative marketed only a few variations. At about that time, however, a virtual "explosion" began with different products, flavors, and packaging. Tree Top already had glass bottles and aluminum cans, but soon started using plastic containers, and later also adopted aseptic (bacteria-free) and similar formats. Plastic packaging, which the cooperative adopted for gallons of juice in 1994, ushered in a new era of containers. The sizes for various containers and products often reflected market forces and consumer

preferences at work. Over time, the shape of bottles became more streamlined and convenient to grasp by hand. Even though the cooperative turned out limited apple juice under several "private labels" for other companies, its own items remained easily identifiable by "Tree Top" in raised lettering on the plastic.

The pattern of Tree Top's workforce has shown an unusual mix of salaried and hourly employees, with the additional feature that some of its plants are unionized and others are not. The Teamsters Union had gained a foothold in Bill Charbonneau's private company and, although the contract supposedly ended with a change of ownership, remained as the bargaining agent with the Tree Top cooperative. As of 2010, the Wenatchee plant as well as the older Selah installation are unionized, while the Ross plant at Selah and the Prosser unit are nonunion. The Cashmere and Rialto, California, plants had also been unionized. For the first 25 years or so, most Tree Top production-line employment was seasonal because the plants stayed open only as long as raw product was available. More recently, the work has been relatively steady, and during harvest time some of the plants have run around the clock.

In the mid-1980s, Tree Top narrowly avoided a strike when negotiations with the Teamsters stalled and the union filed an unfair practices complaint with the National Labor Relations Board. The cooperative, facing increasingly strong market competition from low-priced juice drinks, had asked the union for a 60-cent-per-hour wage reduction. Tree Top also argued that such a concession was reasonable because its employees received noticeably higher wages than those paid in comparable local workplaces. The cooperative won the dispute, in a victory that brought uncertain savings and some resentment among a number of wage earners. In the spring of 2007, during negotiations, the Teamsters did strike at the Rialto installation over the benefits package. The work shutdown possibly might have spread to other unionized Tree Top facilities, but the matter was settled before that occurred.[16]

Tree Top has been successful in attracting and training a specialized and effective workforce. In the early 1980s, the cooperative's vice president for labor relations, Robert E. Hartley, won a national award for promoting a disadvantaged workers program at all the plants. On the organized labor front, as indicated, negotiations with the Teamsters occasionally have been intricate and sometimes

The Rabbis of Prosser

Insects are not kosher. This is why Rabbi Yitzhak Gallor's work begins out in the orchards and fields where fruit and vegetables are grown. This part of his job requires a personal inspection to ensure that a crop destined for the kosher marketplace is free of infestation. Gallor's duties only start with these inspections; he monitors kosher production from harvesting to the grocery store shelves. Altogether, he supervises kosher production done by 97 companies in the Pacific Northwest and Alaska, involving a variety of foods including fruit ingredients, juices, fish, potato commodities, and candy. Besides working with Tree Top, Gallor cooperates with such additional well-known firms as Red Hook, Safeway, Starbucks, Ocean Spray, and others.

In 2009, Gallor's monitoring involved the product lines at all of the Tree Top plants, except the Rialto, Cali-

Vineyards near Prosser.
Joel Magalnick/JTNews, Seattle

fornia, operation where another rabbi was in charge. The Tree Top plant at Prosser is exceptional because it is one of only four facilities in the world where grape processing under kosher supervision runs through the Jewish High Holy Days, seven days a week and around the clock. For the other Tree Top plants, Gallor makes unannounced visits about once a month. At Prosser, he directs a crew of 8 to 12 rabbis remaining onsite throughout the grape harvest, which may last six to eight weeks. These crew members, who often have left wives and families back home, come from virtually every part of the world. During the 2009 harvest, 4 of the 12-member Washington grape crush crew came from Israel; others came from such places as Colorado, New Jersey, Florida, and New York.

Gallor's home base is in Seattle. He and his crew, all Orthodox Jewish rabbis and volunteers, are affiliated with the Union of Orthodox Jewish Congregations of America (OU), a nonprofit organization with headquarters in New York City. To accomplish its objective of making kosher food readily available, the OU gives its stamp of certification (an O encircling a U) to those products that meet its rigid standards. Tree Top contracts with the OU organization, which compensates the rabbis for their services. The OU stamp of certification on specially processed products provides Tree Top access to the kosher market involving billions of dollars. Not only do Orthodox Jews buy these goods, but also Reform and Conservative Jews as well as Seventh-Day Adventists, Muslims, vegetarians, and others with dietary and health concerns. In some large urban centers, consumer preference for kosher foods rivals, or exceeds, the sales of organic products.

At Prosser, observation of grape juice production by Rabbi Gallor and his crew amounts to "kosher quality control." First, their inspections ensure that all of the ingredients, including enzymes and settling agents, come

Rabbi Gallor checking grape processing.
Joel Magalnick/JTNews, Seattle

from vegetarian sources. Second, since Jewish law considers grapes as sacramental fruit, all juice must be heat-treated while monitored by a rabbi. Computers, heat charts, and a seismographic recording device are utilized to assure accuracy. Third, the crew keeps watch on the maze of pipes and feeder lines in the Prosser plant to guarantee that non-kosher ingredients are not mixed in with the kosher product. At the end of production, the rabbis apply a label and tamper-proof seal on the drums, pails, or tanker trucks headed out to the marketplace.[1]

While on assignment at Prosser, the rabbis stay in a nearby motel. Rabbi Gallor notes that the Tree Top management and employees always are congenial and helpful. The rabbis not only have office space in the plant itself, along with a cot, microwave, hot plate, and similar extras, but also receive special attention on Jewish High

Sukkot shelter at Tree Top.
Joel Magalnick/JTNews, Seattle

Holy Days. For instance, the eight-day Jewish holiday of Sukkot commemorates the 40 years the ancient Israelites wandered in the desert after the Exodus from Egypt. Reminiscent of the Exodus lifestyle, Orthodox Jews live and eat during Sukkot, as prescribed by holy writ, in a makeshift structure with a bamboo roof. Tree Top has made such a structure available at Prosser. The Prosser facility is known for its versatility—for the variety of fruits handled to the different methods of processing performed—and the unusual work of the kosher rabbis is one more proof of this point.

---

1. For an account of Rabbi Gallor's activities, see "Stomping Good Job," *Jewish Transcript* (Seattle), October 15, 2009, online. A pamphlet, *The OU Guide to Preparing Fruits and Vegetables* (New York: Orthodox Union, 2004), provides guidelines for kosher inspection procedures regarding these products.

---

hit a snag as would be expected in such arrangements, but Tree Top has never suffered shutdown by a strike.[17] Health insurance and retirement plans in all the plants and corporate units have helped retain skilled workers and administrators. In the various communities, job openings at Tree Top installations have ordinarily attracted a waiting line of applicants. An unusual number of workers and administrators have been with the firm for between 20 and 30 years, and appointments to management positions have frequently come from within the company's ranks. Characteristically, long-time employees express their personal pride in Tree Top's national and worldwide accomplishments.

These expressions of individual pride, as well as Tree Top's imprinted slogan "Real Fruit from Real People," help explain the overall success of this agricultural cooperative. For 50 years, the board of directors and management teams have made strategic adjustments and policy-making decisions to meet the challenges of powerful private competitors and foreign governments. By the late 20th century, some experts questioned whether agricultural cooperatives could survive in a world of multinational corporations and cartels.

The only way, some specialists observed, was to grow in size and "increase the scope of the business" in matching proportions. Tree Top was cited as a prime example—"the nation's biggest apple processor," and "now an international concern, selling its industrial products…to 26 countries."[18] Flexibility, toughness, and dedication to sound business principles were required in the modern age, but the pride of personal involvement remained equally important.

Naturally, the Tree Top management team always has been on the lookout for ways to serve and attract the consuming public. On the other side of the coin, most grocery store customers probably do not realize how often they are using the cooperative's products. A Yakima trade publication explained why: "You may be eating Tree Top products without knowing it. The blueberry muffin you had with breakfast? Chances are pretty good that the bits of 'blueberry' were actually dried, flavored apple chunks from Tree Top." The same could be said for the "strawberry" flakes found in instant oatmeal. Even a close reading of the label on a name-brand steak sauce may reveal apple concentrate included in the ingredients. Because apple components are tasty, cheaper, and readily absorb other fruit flavors, many

Alphabetical Listing of Members of the Board of Directors

Board member have always served three years terms, beginning immediately upon election as determined by a tally of votes cast by the grower-members. Since the announcement of election centers on the date of the annual meeting, the exact dates of their terms are determined accordingly. However, in 1972 the annual meeting was changed from March to November, and in that year the membership met and announced elections in both months. Historical sources for the early 1960s are somewhat incomplete and leave question about the exact dates of some early board members' terms. Tree Top Bylaws prescribe that the board shall consist of 12 members, with 6 elected from the Northern District and 6 from the Southern District. The dividing line between the districts is U.S. Interstate 90, which runs east-west and crosses the Columbia River at Vantage, Washington. The hometowns listed below are all in Washington. Members of the original board that incorporated the Tree Top cooperative are denoted by an asterisk (*).

Bruce Allen, Yakima, 1994–Present
Tom Auvil, Orondo, 1988–Present
John Borton, Yakima, 1986–2004
Hubert W. Burnett, Chelan, 1960–83*
Grant M. Call, Tonasket, 1960–72*
George Chapman, Brewster, 1981–2006
John Clayton, Orondo, 1986–94
Ray Colbert, Tonasket, 1972–Present
Darrell Collins, Monitor, 1990–2005
Roy E. Coulthard, Cashmere, 1960–75*
Dick Cowin, Wapato, 1987–Present
Harold Cozart, Chelan, 1983–86
Robert Crossland, Grandview, 1962–75
Guido Deiro, Yakima, 1969–74
A.T. "Thor" Fossum, Yakima, 1960–84*
Herbert L. Frank, Yakima, 1963–64(?)
Cragg Gilbert, Yakima, 1974–86
Robert Hartley, Manson, 1960–62*
Marvin Jeffries, Manson, 1983–88
Ray Keller, Gleed/Yakima, 1987–Present
Ed Kershaw, Yakima, 2004–Present
John Mazie, Cowiche, 1984–87
Dean Monroe, Bridgeport, 1973–82

Victor Morgan, Omak, 1960–73*
Warren Morgan, Quincy, 2006–Present
Wilbur Nelson, Cowiche, 1966–83
Dick Olsen, Prosser, 1988–2006
Larry Olsen, Prosser, 1981–87
Raymond O'Neal, Chelan, 1962–83
Orville Ormiston, Yakima, 1960–81*
David Parsons, Leavenworth, 1974–83
Donald Paton, Cashmere, 1961(?)–74
Sid Perkins, Wenatchee, 1975–82
Charles Peters, Wapato, 1976–94
Otis Riggs, Wapato, 1960–75*
Desmond Shearer, Tieton, 1960–66*
Michael Smith, Yakima, 2006–Present
Randy Smith, Cashmere, 2006–Present
Doug Stockwell, Bridgeport, 1994–Present
Charles B. Stoll, Yakima, 1960–62(?)*
Ralph Strand, Cowiche, 1960–63*
Roger Strand, Cowiche, 1983–Present
Fred Valentine, East Wenatchee, 1983–Present
Peter Van Well, Wenatchee, 1979–90
James Welch Jr., East Wenatchee, 1960–61(?)*
John White, Grandview, 1975–88

companies opt to make the savings, and indeed correctly claim that the contents contain "Pure Fruit."[19]

From the beginning, the people who counted the most and who had given Tree Top the reason to exist were its members. The cooperative has served growers well by expanding into innovative markets, acquiring additional production facilities, turning out a steady stream of new products, and remaining always alert to maintain the highest

level of operational efficiency—all to provide the orchardists with higher-than-market prices for their cull fruit.

Raw statistics seldom tell the whole story, but even so, they are informative. In the years following the Alar alarm, the record of prices paid for raw product shows ups and downs, but overall, membership in the cooperative provided growers with a reliable market and steady income. In 1990, Tree Top received about 375,000 member and nonmember tonnages of apples and pears; 10 years before, it was 170,000 tons. In 1990, sales were about $268 million and the per ton return to growers on peelers was $108, juice fruit $57, and pears $35. By 2008, the total tons received was about 267,000, although the seven-year average was about 401,000 tons. Significantly, despite the smaller tonnage in 2008, sales that year of more than $295 million were the highest in that seven year period, as were the member proceeds at $209 per ton for peelers, $188 for juice fruit, and $54 for pears. From 2002 to 2008, the average per ton paid to members for peelers was about $112, for juice fruit about $74, and for pears about $38. In short, being reliable and steady are the operative terms for the role the Tree Top cooperative has fulfilled in serving its grower-members.

The historical importance of Tree Top in the overall Washington state apple industry can be pinpointed by a single visual image. It is the large picture covering most of a page in *Life* magazine in 1951, depicting 3,200 carloads of Washington apples disposed of at the Yakima city dump since there was no market for them. *Life* showed a bulldozer shoving "the newest apple glut…into a deep fermenting carpet, seven acres in area." Pigs rooted around in the discards, which had been valued at $6 million dollars earlier in the year.[20] As explained previously, many growers were paying $5 a ton to have their culls hauled away to the dump or selling them at a loss for cattle feed. The only returns orchardists got then were "the flies who soon returned from the dump to pester households in the area."[21]

After the formation of the Tree Top cooperative in 1960, the grower-members had a lucrative outlet for their culls and received substantial monetary returns. Tree Top helped complete the Washington apple industry's structure by furnishing a bottom tier derived from the one-fourth of each crop's sortouts at the warehouses. Later the cooperative opened a similar processing market for pears and pear remnants, which were used primarily in blends and as a natural sweetener generally.

In 1975, Victor Morgan, an early "president" of the Tree Top board, and a board member for 13 years, reminisced about his long career as an orchardist in the Okanogan country. Morgan believed he had seen three major events transform the Washington apple industry—the switch from individual apple boxes to bins, the introduction of controlled atmosphere storage (CA), and the formation

and success of the Tree Top cooperative. Much of a grower's time in harvesting apples had been spent in moving boxes around. Then, Morgan said, came bins that held 25 boxes of fruit and could be moved by fork lifts. CA took care of storage for year-around marketing, especially in years with bumper crops, but there was always the problem of culls, or sortouts, unsuitable for the fresh-fruit trade. The third major event, Morgan believed, was the success of Tree Top in providing a "home" for the lowly culls and putting substantial extra money into growers' pockets. As a bonus, the cooperative had helped keep the fresh-apple market "steady" by using a formerly unwanted surplus, and thereby boosting overall prices.[22]

Several years later, one of Victor Morgan's successors as the board of directors chairman explained it in different terms. Raymond C. O'Neal aptly described Tree Top's importance in the number one apple-growing state this way: "We've put a floor under the fresh apple market where none had previously existed. Tree Top has [also] successfully developed the processing pear, just as it did the processing apple." Randy Smith, another board member and prominent industry leader, went even further, commenting that the pricing involved with Tree Top and other processors actually set the base price for the fresh-apple market. A Seattle newspaper described the role played by processors as a "safety net."[23] Regardless of the terminology, without a stabilizing floor the overall price structure undoubtedly would have sunk to a lower level. The comparison to a "floor," or an essential "foundation stone," still holds true on the 50th anniversary of Tree Top Inc.—a national and international pacesetter in a global industry. 🍎

Endnotes

1. Besides concentrate storage, the Prosser plant has the most diverse capabilities of all the Tree Top installations, producing purees, blends, both frozen and single strength juice, and apple and pear concentrate.
2. *Yakima Herald-Republic*, October 28, 2008, online. Sabroso joined Northwest Naturals as one of Tree Top's two wholly owned but independently operated subsidiaries.
3. Jacquelyn Mitchard, "The Search for the Perfect Apple," *Parade*, August 30, 2009. This widely circulated "magazine" is inserted in many Sunday newspaper editions.
4. In some cases, the new orchards contained more than 2,000 dwarf variety trees per acre. To plant that many trees, it was necessary to space them one or two feet apart and install supporting

wires, which gave the appearance of something like a vineyard, only taller. The new varieties came into production within two or three years, instead of the previous seven or more years for maturity.

5. David Lester, "Apple Prices Drop amid Record Crop," *Spokane Spokesman-Review*, April 9, 2009, A8.

6. This product has a trademark registration with the lower case "t," and thus is marketed as "trim," obviously to emphasize its weight control potential.

7. The connection between market rights and membership was an essential feature of the cooperative's organizational structure. In 1986, with excess inventories on hand, Tree Top had attempted to limit membership by decreeing that growers could no longer become members by purchasing market rights from the cooperative itself, but could do so only by buying the market rights of current or retiring members.

8. CEO Tom Stokes explained the new system to Tree Top employees in *Apple Corps*, January 2009.

9. Because of the influx of cheap foreign concentrate, the United States now produces substantially less of it than previously. Tree Top still makes concentrate, but only for its own use.

10. For earlier methods of cold storage and refrigeration, see Amanda L. Van Lanen, "'We Have Grown Fine Fruit Whether We Would or No': The History of the Washington State Apple Industry, 1880–1930," Ph.D. dissertation, Washington State University, 2009, 115–23.

11. For an example of the eulogies to CA and its founders, see *Yakima Morning Herald*, March 18, 1966, 1. Improvements to CA have extended the shelf life and enhanced the firmness and flavor of fruit that otherwise does not store well. As one of the varieties with a relatively short storage life, Red Delicious apples have especially benefitted from CA updating.

12. See A. Desmond O'Rourke, *The World Apple Market* (New York: Food Products Press, 1994), 3–5, 8–9. In Tree Top's current processing operations, the mainstays as peelers for ingredients include such varieties as Golden Delicious, Fuji, and Granny Smith. For apple sauce, Romes are essential, and for juices, all the varieties. High acidity in blending calls for Granny Smith, Pink Lady, and Braeburns. The delivery of specific varieties is determined by the product being manufactured at a given time.

13. "Tree Top Still Hoping Its Blend Will Soak Up Big Share of Market—Three Apple Blend," *Yakima Herald-Republic*, March 31, 1999, 1B.

14. *Apple Corps*, February 1997, March 1998. See also, Capps, et al., *Contributions of Nonalcoholic Beverages to the U.S. Diet* (USDA, Economic Research Service, 2005), which compiles statistics on the selection and at-home consumption of various beverages, including fruit juices and fruit drinks, based on race and ethnicity, income level, household size, educational level, and other factors.

15. *Apple Corps*, August 1999, April 2000.

16. Associated Press dispatch, *Spokane Chronicle*, November 21, 1985; *Wenatchee World*, May 17, 2007—both online.

17. On the disadvantaged workers program, see *Tree Topics*, December 1970, April 1981. For an example of labor negotiations, the Teamsters in 2006 won an arbitrated dispute with Tree Top over the payment of extra overtime. *Labor Law Developments*, Winter 2007, online. When the Cashmere plant closed, the Teamsters contested some of the terms offered to discharged employees. See *Wenatchee World*, December 7, 2007, online.

18. Bill Virgin, "Co-Ops Keep Pace in Business World: Member-owned Groups Adjust to Changing Economic Role," *Seattle Post Intelligencer*, September 7, 1993, B8.

19. *Yakima Valley Business Times*, May 11, 2001, B-5.

20. "Sad Applesauce: Glut Ends in a $6 Million Mess," *Life*, September 10, 1951.

21. *Tree Topics*, January 22, 1973.

22. Morgan interviewed in the *Omak Chronicle*, February 6, 1975.

23. Randy Smith interviewed in the *Wenatchee World*, October 3, 1999, B1; *Seattle Times*, October 3, 1999—both online.

Acknowledgments

First, I wish to thank Amanda L. Van Lanen for her valuable help in the research and writing of *Tree Top: Creating a Fruit Revolution*. During this project, she was completing a doctoral dissertation on the history of the Washington apple industry. As the endnotes in the preceding pages indicate, much of her work made a perfect fit regarding Tree Top's background and heritage. In addition, she did a professional job in organizing corporate records and archives, as well as the cooperative's historical files and photographs. Throughout the project, she demonstrated her scholarly insights and editorial skills. Tree Top Inc. provided a significant contribution to higher education and historical study related to the state's apple industry by funding a research assistantship for the last year of Dr. Van Lanen's graduate program.

I also want to thank all the people at Tree Top for their cooperation and encouragement. At the risk of overlooking some of that large number, I will start with Tom Stokes, president and CEO, who took time to explain a number of operational details and clarify some of my conceptions. Others who provided the same service included Laura Prisc, former corporate communications manager, as well as her successor, Sharon Miracle; Nancy Buck, vice president of legal services; Lindsay Buckner, senior vice president of field services; Diana Roeber, administrative assistant to the president; and Robert Payne, graphic artist. Plant managers and other personnel at the various facilities who gave me informative tours or helpful explanations include (at the two Selah plants) Mike Fausto, Tim Evans, Rick Templeton, and Chris Breese; (at Wenatchee) Joe Brooks and Sarah Hermann; (at Cashmere) Mark Burnett; and (at Prosser) Gary Stapleton and Dallas McCauley. I need to emphasize, however, that none of these good folks can be held accountable for how I might have used their information in this book.

The following individuals, who gave me the benefit of their knowledge and experience in extended comments, have my deep appreciation: Tom Auvil, Ray Keller, and Randy Smith, present board members; George Chapman, former board member; Robert M. "Bob" Dennis, former vice president of field services; Max L. Steward, Gleed orchardist; Letty Ann Ginn and West Campbell, daughter and grandson of Clifford A. Ross; Rabbi Yitzhak Gallor, coordinator of the rabbis at Prosser; and Pat Moss, former Tree Top corporate communications manager, who indeed "went the extra mile" in providing assistance.

In the process of gathering information and illustrations, several persons made special efforts to provide what I requested: Sally A. King, art curator, BNSF Railway Company Archives, Fort Worth, Texas; Gus Melonas, BNSF regional director of public affairs, Seattle; (in Vancouver, Washington) Jessica Antoine, city forestry outreach coordinator, and Donna Howard Jacky and her father, Elwin Howard; Larry Kangas, mural artist, Beaverton, Oregon; Robert West, photographer, Milwaukie, Oregon; Chris Maple, graphic artist, Olympia; John Auvil, Auvil Fruit Company, Orondo. I also want to thank professional transcription specialists Teresa Bergen, Portland, and Susan Walling, Vancouver, for their good work.

At Washington State University, Pullman, I owe a huge debt of gratitude to Patricia Thorsten-Mickleson, finance/personnel manager, College of Liberal Arts, for all the ways she has helped me in this project. Others at WSU who provided valuable advice and assistance included Susan Cunnington, CLA grant coordinator; and Erin Rice and Carrie Johnston, grant and research coordinators, Office of Grant and Research Development. My special thanks go to those at the WSU Press who were always considerate and helpful no matter what the situation happened to be: Mary Read, director; Glen Lindeman, editor-in-chief; Kerry Darnall, copy editor; Nancy Grunewald, layout designer; Jean Taylor, publications coordinator; and Caryn Lawton, marketing coordinator.

Undoubtedly, many others deserve mentioning. Please accept my apologies for anyone I have overlooked.

David H. Stratton
Pullman, Washington

Bibliography

Company Records

Unless cited otherwise, most of the information used in this book was obtained from the Tree Top Inc. Historical Files, which were deposited for the duration of the project in the Departmental Archives, Department of History, Washington State University, Pullman. This collection consists of a wide variety of source material, such as company publications, annual reports, specialized studies, media releases, board of directors' minutes, financial reports, advertising material, and photographs of people and events. Of special importance in these files is a typewritten manuscript, "Tree Top—The Story of Apple Juice." Although no author is listed, this historical account was written in the 1970s by Ernest L. "Ernie" Stafford, a retired Tree Top executive. Also, longtime corporate communications manager Patricia Gail "Pat" Moss conducted interviews in the 1980s and early 2000s with past and present board members, as well as other knowledgeable persons. Along with research in company records and other sources, Moss used the interview transcripts to compile a typewritten history of Tree Top on file cards. Access to the Tree Top Inc. Historical Files is restricted under privacy and company confidentiality regulations.

Apple Corps (employees newsletter)—July 1992, January/February 1995, Spring 1995, September/October 1995, November/December 1995, January/February 1996, February 1997, June 1997, February 1998, March 1988, January 1994, April 1998, August 1999, January 2000, April 2000, May 2000, November 2000, May 2001, September 2003, March 2004, January 2009.

Moss, Pat. Historical records on typewritten 4 X 6½ inch file cards, 1980s–early 2000s.

[Stafford, Ernest L.] "Tree Top—The Story of Apple Juice." Typewritten manuscript, ca. 1970s.

Tree Top Annual Reports—1973 to 2009.

Tree Topics (members newsletter)—September 30, 1968, December 1970, June 1972, January 1973, April 1973, December 1973, March 1974, October 1977, December 1978, June 1980, February 1981, April 1981, December 1981, November 1982, October 1984, November 1984, April 1985, March/April 1986, May 1986, October 1986, April 1987, August/September 1987, October/November 1987, May/June 1988, December 1988, January 1994, October 2002, February 2003.

Bulletins and Reports

Caldwell, J.S. "Evaporation of Apples," Bulletin 131. Pullman: Agricultural Experiment Station, State College of Washington, May 1916.

Calvin, Linda, and Barry Krissoff. "Resolution of the U.S.-Japan Apple Dispute: New Opportunities for Trade," Outlook Report No. FTS31801. Washington, D.C.: U.S. Department of Agriculture, Economic Research Service, October 2005. www.ers.usda.gov/Publications/FTS/oct05/FTS31801.

Capps, Oral, Jr., Annette Clauson, Joanne Guthrie, Grant Pittman, and Matthew Stockton. *Contributions of Nonalcoholic Beverages to the U.S. Diet.* Economic Research Report No. 1. Washington, D.C.: U.S. Department of Agriculture, Economic Research Service, 2005.

Greig, W. Smith. "Location Advantages in Applesauce Processing in the U.S. with Some Implications for the Washington Apple Industry," Bulletin 753. Pullman: Washington Agricultural Experiment Station, Washington State University, 1972.

_____, and Leroy L. Blakeslee, "Potentials for Apple Juice Processing in the U.S. with Implications for Washington," Bulletin 808. Pullman: College of Agriculture Research Center, Washington State University, April 1975.

O'Rourke, A. Desmond. *The Washington Apple Industry to the Year 2000.* Information Series No. 58. Pullman: IMPACT Center, College of Agriculture and Home Economics, Washington State University, February 1993.

Court Cases

Auvil v. CBS "60 Minutes" 800 F. Supp. 928 (E.D. Wash. 06/05/1992).

Hunt v. Washington State Apple Advertising Commission 432 U.S. 333 (1997).

Dissertations and Thesis

Cho, Sung-Yeol. "An Economic Analysis of the Washington Apple Industry." Ph.D. dissertation, Washington State University, 2004.

Neubert, Alfred Max. "A Study of the Effect of Filtration, Clarification, and Concentration on the Composition and Properties of Apple Juice." Ph.D. dissertation, State College of Washington, 1941.

Sharkasi, Tawfix Y. "Dilution and Solids Adulteration of Apple Juice." M.S. thesis, Washington State University, 1979.

Van Lanen, Amanda L. "'We Have Grown Fine Fruit Whether We Would or No': The History of the Washington State Apple Industry, 1880–1930." Ph.D. dissertation, Washington State University, 2009.

Zaragoza, Tony. "Apple Capital: Growers, Labor, and Technology in the Origin and Development of the Washington State Apple Industry, 1890–1930." Ph.D. dissertation, Washington State University, 2007.

Journals, Magazines, and Periodicals

American/Western Fruit Grower. September 1983.

Bloom, Stephen G. "The New Pioneers." *Wilson Quarterly* 30 (Summer 2006).

Consumer Reports. "Alar: Not Gone, Not Forgotten," 54, no. 5 (May 1989) (online).

_____. "No More Bad Apples," 55, no. 7 (July 1990).

Ellison, Joseph W. "The Beginnings of the Apple Industry in Oregon." *Agricultural History* 11 (October 1937).

————. "The Cooperative Movement in the Oregon Apple Industry, 1910–1929." *Agricultural History* 13 (April 1939).

Freeman, Otis W. "Apple Industry of the Wenatchee Area." *Economic Geography* 10 (April 1934).

(The) Goodfruit Grower. December 1, 1967.

————. May 1, 1978.

————. April 1, 2009.

Guterson, David. "The Kingdom of Apples: Picking the Fruit of Immortality in Washington's Laden Orchards." *Harper's Magazine,* October 1999.

Letters to the Editor. *Columbia Journalism Review* 35 (November/ December 1996).

Life. "Sad Applesauce: Glut Ends in a $6 Million Mess," September 10, 1951.

McClintock, Thomas C. "Henderson Luelling, Seth Lewelling, and the Birth of the Pacific Coast Fruit Industry." *Oregon Historical Quarterly* 68 (June 1967).

Mitchard, Jacquelyn. "The Search for the Perfect Apple." *Parade,* August 30, 2009.

Negin, Elliott. "The Alar 'Scare' Was for Real; and So Is that 'Veggie Hate-Crime' Movement." *Columbia Journalism Review* 35 (September/October 1996) and (November/December 1986).

Newsweek. "How Safe Is Your Food?" March 27, 1989.

Time. "Is Anything Safe? How Two Tainted Grapes Triggered a Panic about What We Eat," March 27, 1989.

Monographs and Books

Biggs, Gilbert W. *Cooperatives in the Apple Industry.* Cooperative Marketing and Purchasing Division, Agricultural Cooperative Service, U.S. Department of Agriculture, Washington, D.C., September 1987.

Eisen, Yosef, et al. *The OU Guide to Preparing Fruits and Vegetables.* New York: Orthodox Union, 2004.

Ficken, Robert E. *Washington State: The Inaugural Decade, 1889–1899.* Pullman: Washington State University Press, 2007.

Johansen, Dorothy O., and Charles M. Gates. *Empire of the Columbia: A History of the Pacific Northwest.* 2nd ed. New York: Harper and Row, 1967.

LeWarne, Charles P. *Washington State.* Seattle: University of Washington Press, 1986.

Lince, Robert S. *The Selah Story: History of Selah, East Selah, and Wenas Valley in Yakima County, Washington.* Selah: Selah Valley Optimist Printing, 1984.

Meinig, D.W. *The Great Columbia Plain: A Historical Geography, 1805–1910.* Seattle: University of Washington Press, 1968.

O'Rourke, A. Desmond. *The World Apple Market.* New York: Food Products Press, 1994.

Price, Robert. *Johnny Appleseed: Man and Myth.* Bloomington: Indiana University Press, 1954.

Schwantes, Carlos A. *The Pacific Northwest: An Interpretive History.* Rev. ed. Lincoln: University of Nebraska Press, 1989.

Scott, James W. *Washington: A Centennial Atlas.* Bellingham: Center for Pacific Northwest Studies, Western Washington University, 1989.

Stratton, David H., ed. *Washington Comes of Age: The State in the National Experience.* Pullman: Washington State University Press, 1992.

Unruh, John D., Jr. *The Plains Across: The Overland Emigrants and the Trans-Mississippi West, 1840–60.* Urbana: University of Illinois Press, 1979.

Newspapers

Dallas Morning News. December 8, 2007 (online).

Jewish Transcript. October 15, 2009 (online).

New York Times. March 24, 1989 (online), November 29, 1990 (online), July 9, 1991 (online), July 1, 2007 (online).

Omak Chronicle. February 6, 1975.

Prosser Record-Bulletin. June 28, 1979.

Puget Sound Business Journal. July 2, 1990 (online), June 24, 1999, November 10, 2003 (online).

Seattle Post-Intelligencer. September 2, 1987, February 16, 1988, March 1, 1989, March 17, 1989, May 24, 1989, May 27, 1989, June 1, 1989, June 3, 1989, September 7, 1993, October 2, 1995 (online), February 27, 1996, September 20, 1999.

Seattle Times. March 16, 1988, May 24, 1989, June 1, 1989, June 15, 1989, January 22, 1990 (online), June 9, 1990 (online), July 1, 1991 (online), November 26, 1991 (online), February 19, 1995, October 3, 1999 (online), April 8, 2000 (online), October 14, 2002, June 23, 2005, September 4, 2005 (online).

Selah Valley Optimist. July 9, 1936, March 18, 1937, July 27, 1937, October 12, 1944.

Spokane Chronicle. November 21, 1985 (online).

Spokane Spokesman-Review. April 9, 2009.

Vancouver Columbian. October 2, 2009, October 4, 2009.

Wall Street Journal. October 3, 1989 (online).

Wenatchee World. October 14, 1993 (online), October 3, 1999 (online), May 17, 2007 (online), December 7, 2007 (online).

Yakima Herald-Republic. April 12, 1978, March 31, 1999, May 3, 2008, October 28, 2008 (online).

Yakima Herald-Tribune. October 24, 1996, September 17, 1999, November 7, 2003.

Yakima Morning Herald. March 20, 1963, March 18, 1966.

Yakima Valley Business Times. May 11, 2001.

Other Sources

Labor Law Developments. Winter 2007 (online).

Office of the U.S. Trade Representative, press release, June 23, 2005 (online).

U.S. Apple Association, news release, November 19, 2002.

Vancouver-Clark County Parks and Recreation Website, October 27, 2009.

Index